I. E. Diekenga

Daniel Poldertot

I. E. Diekenga

Daniel Poldertot

ISBN/EAN: 9783743373792

Manufactured in Europe, USA, Canada, Australia, Japa

Cover: Foto ©ninafisch / pixelio.de

Manufactured and distributed by brebook publishing software (www.brebook.com)

I. E. Diekenga

Daniel Poldertot

UNCLE DAN POLDERTOT GOING TO MARKET. — Page 28.

A Story,

WHEREIN IS CAREFULLY RECORDED THE INTERESTING
ADVENTURES OF

UNCLE DAN AND HIS FAITHFUL FRIENDS

MR. ROBERT STURDY, MR. HARRY CRIBBLER,
AND MR. RICHARD DOOLITTLE.

BY

I. E. DIEKENGA.

BOSTON:
JAMES H. EARLE, PUBLISHER,
178 WASHINGTON STREET.
1882.

Copyright, 1882,
By I. E. DIEKENGA.

BOSTON:
W. F. BROWN AND COMPANY, PRINTERS,
218 FRANKLIN ST.

BOSTON STEREOTYPE FOUNDRY,
No. 4 PEARL STREET.

PREFACE.

IT is with the heartiest pleasure and satisfaction that Mr. Daniel Poldertot — otherwise familiarly known as Uncle Dan — is herewith presented to an admiring and appreciative public.

I have the fullest confidence that, wherever his rotund form and smiling countenance are seen, he will be welcomed and received with the delight and enthusiasm to which the genial qualities of his head and heart entitle him. And those discontented and envious people, if any such there be, who dare to gloomily assert that Uncle Dan is neither a great man nor a wise one will be consigned to merited oblivion by a discriminating and indignant community. As to Uncle Dan's friends, I confess to a special interest in their history, seeing that it perpetuates to some degree the light-hearted happiness and good humor of a time that was particularly bright and pleasant.

Thus, while writing it, I distinctly participated in the exercises of the Band of Hope, and pressed, involuntarily, the very streets traversed by Uncle Dan and his devoted friends, while a feeling of intimate acquaintance with every scene, of happy familiarity with every character, took entire possession of me; so that I even saw the old tin sign revolving on its rusty iron rod near Dr. Bulbous' door, and laughed more than once as Mr. Bromley started off in hot pursuit after his friend, the aggravating Mr. Seldon.

Under this feeling the story has naturally assumed its present character, and I truly hope the company of Uncle Dan and his merry companions will prove as pleasant and agreeable to others as it has to me.

I. E. DIEKENGA.

CONTENTS.

CHAPTER I.
Which has the honor of introducing the amiable Mr. Poldertot and his very excellent wife; and describes how the meditations of the former were unexpectedly interrupted 11

CHAPTER II.
The distressing occurrences connected with the purchase of vegetables; showing the extraordinary facility possessed by Uncle Dan for getting into trouble, and how he got out of it 28

CHAPTER III.
Which, besides containing a description of Mr. Poldertot's establishment, embraces the record of the marvellous disappearance of a suit of clothes, and finally tells what became of it 41

CHAPTER IV.
Introducing two great geniuses (although as yet unknown to fame) who are destined to frequently reappear in these pages. — A perplexity. — A bright idea . . 49

CHAPTER V.
A mysterious communication, which causes a noble resolution to animate the heart of Uncle Dan 57

CHAPTER VI.

A peculiar street and the peculiar transactions which took place upon it, including the peculiar actions of a peculiar sign 66

CHAPTER VII.

In which Mr. Robert Sturdy is lamentably unsuccessful, and Mr. Brankey comes to grief 81

CHAPTER VIII.

Mr. Poldertot is surprised in more ways than one, and Mr. Sluff develops talent as an orator under unusual circumstances 94

CHAPTER IX.

Mr. Doolittle again assists Uncle Dan, and, sociably inclined, interviews Mr. Rolf Seppeld 111

CHAPTER X.

The exciting adventures connected with the loss of a turtle-dove 124

CHAPTER XI.

Wherein is described the satisfactory though wholly unexpected manner in which Uncle Dan's advertisement is answered 139

CHAPTER XII.

Which begins with anticipations, continues with apprehension, and ends with joy — all upon the part of Uncle Dan 145

CHAPTER XIII.

Mr. Poldertot and his friends meet in order to leave the city together. — A very nice young lady. — The arrival of Mr. Krowps 161

CHAPTER XIV.

Mr. Krowps converses sociably, and expatiates upon the virtues of tooth-powders 170

CHAPTER XV.

Which records not only the extremely novel and highly interesting exercises of Uncle Dan and his companions, but also the gloomy political reflections of the astute Mr. Krowps 175

CHAPTER XVI.

A warm welcome. — The meeting of Uncle Dan and Aunt Prudence 181

CHAPTER XVII.

The painful result of Mr. Doolittle's pugilistic dreams, and Mr. Poldertot's eloquent plea in behalf of the innocent creatures of the forest 186

CHAPTER XVIII.

How the visitors hunted. — Mr. Sturdy's vain-glorious boasting and his ignominious failure. — The fruitlessness of Uncle Dan's benevolent intentions, and his consequent grief 193

CHAPTER XIX.

An invitation to attend a festival, and how Uncle Dan was compelled to go 204

CHAPTER XX.

The renowned individuals who greeted Uncle Dan; and the impressions created by the gallant Mr. Sturdy and the polite Mr. Cribbler 209

CHAPTER XXI.

Wherein is related how Mr. Robert Sturdy interrupted the peaceful conversation of the most distinguished people in the world, and invoked the protection of the law 221

CHAPTER XXII.

How Mr. Sturdy disappointed the law and the people. — His extraordinary and distressing adventures in the dark 227

CHAPTER XXIII.

Dick tells Uncle Dan a strange piece of news. — The lost girl. — "She must be found" 234

CHAPTER XXIV.

Mr. Cliphart is herewith presented, and announces an approaching serenade 248

CHAPTER XXV.

A mysterious shadow, and a silent watcher 254

CHAPTER XXVI.

The beginning of the serenade 257

CHAPTER XXVII.

The wonderful serenade 261

CHAPTER XXVIII.

Which is chiefly remarkable as showing Mr. Brankey's great respect for Prof. Bulbous, as presenting Mr. Cliphart in the *role* of a peacemaker, and as dissolving a mysterious shadow into equally mysterious flame 268

CHAPTER XXIX.

Uncle Dan prepares to receive expected visitors, and receives two who were not expected 275

CHAPTER XXX.

The inexplicable absence of Mr. Richard Doolittle continues; and, on the contrary, Mr. William Bromley and Mr. Ben Seldon put in an appearance in their usual quiet and harmonious manner. — A summons for Aunt Prudence. — A very unsatisfactory tea . . 281

CHAPTER XXXI.

The success of Mr. Doolittle's endeavors. — The lost found, and the extraordinary antics indulged in upon this occasion by the overjoyed Mr. Poldertot . . . 290

CHAPTER XXXII.

In which some matters which have hitherto been secrets are explained. — A startling appeal 298

CHAPTER XXXIII.

Which relates how Mr. Sturdy set out to punish the false professor; why he did not do it, and ends with his commendable determination to comfort a young lady 307

CHAPTER XXXIV.

Uncle Dan to the rescue. — The story of the false friend.
— The mob 311

CHAPTER XXXV.

The heroic action of Uncle Dan and his friends. — The alarming manifestations in a coal cellar. — A strange mishap to Mr. Sturdy succeeded by success and joy. — The last of the old tin sign. 316

CHAPTER XXXVI.

Which is the last of all, and contains the natural conclusion of all that has gone before, namely, the end . 337

UNCLE DAN.

CHAPTER I.

Which has the honor of introducing the amiable Mr. Poldertot and his very excellent wife, and describes how the meditations of the former were unexpectedly disturbed.

N a bright, sunny morning in the month of September there appeared in one of the second story windows of a house on Benton street, in the city of St. Louis, a round, ruddy, and unusually pleasant face.

This face, upon which there rested an expression of the greatest satisfaction and good nature, turned slowly in a hollow receptacle composed of the upturned palms of a pair of broad and chubby hands, from left to right and from right to left, and was thus successively presented to the west, the north, and the east, and, *vice versa*, to the east, the north, and the west.

The round, ruddy face which was beaming in this pleasant manner upon the surrounding neighborhood belonged to a stout, middle-aged gentleman, who was gracefully balanced with his elbows upon the window-sill, and his knees upon a cane-bottomed chair.

He was clad in a shirt of immaculate whiteness, a brown vest, which adhered closely to his well-developed form, and a pair of checked trousers, which were so extraordinarily wide and had so much room to spare that they looked as if they might have been intended for one of the ancient giants.

As this stout, middle-aged gentleman looked blandly forth, he moved his body gently, causing the chair upon which his knees were supported to tilt over and to rock slowly back and forth with an easy, gliding motion before the window.

This gentleman was Mr. Poldertot, known far and wide by common consent as Uncle Dan; and in this picturesque attitude Uncle Dan was contemplating the beauties of nature — and of art, — as they lay stretched out before him; — and waiting for his breakfast.

It cannot be strenuously asserted that these beauties of nature, — and of art, — were deserving of any great degree of admiration or attention; but, at the same time, it cannot be denied that Uncle Dan bestowed upon them, with the greatest pleasure, an attention which was undivided and an admiration which was undisguised.

The scene which was thus the subject of Uncle Dan's pleasant observation comprised a view of Benton street; to the right until several stunted and dust-covered locust-trees impeded the sight, and to the left for a distance of five hundred feet, where a sudden, provoking, and wholly unaccountable turn in the street shut off the perspective, and confined the view in that direction to a few old weather-beaten stables. Across the way stood a large, square, old-fashioned, double brick house, surrounded by an open space which had probably once been a garden, but which now could only boast the presence of a few sickly rose and lilac-bushes and a remarkably healthy crop of weeds; and beyond the open space could be seen the usual city panorama of roofs, chimneys, telegraph-poles, lightning-rods, garret-windows, and church-steeples.

It is quite uncertain how much time Uncle Dan might have spent in the contemplation of these delightful scenes had he not experienced an interruption to his observations. For, just as the cane-bottomed chair was moving forward for the fiftieth time, and at the moment that a peculiarly happy smile was beginning to overspread his pleasant, ruddy countenance, Uncle Dan experienced a sudden, sharp, and wholly unexpected sensation in his left arm, which instantly changed the whole current of his thoughts, and transformed the happy smile into an expression of the keenest pain.

At the same time Uncle Dan moved so violently and quickly back from the window, that the chair, overcome by the shock, slipped from under him, precipitating the astonished Mr. Poldertot to the floor beneath the window-sill, from whence he rolled helplessly into a recess between the sofa and the wall.

"Dear me!" said Uncle Dan, as soon as he had recovered sufficient breath to utter an exclamation. "Dear me!"

"Now, then!" said another voice in a tone of sharp impatience, "*will* you hear me, sir? *Will* you answer me when I call again?"

Uncle Dan, thus rudely accosted, looked up with an air of helpless bewilderment, and became conscious of the presence of a tall, slim lady, whose prominent characteristics were a dark brown calico dress profusely illustrated with dots, a blue flannel cape, a white lace cap, and a face whose extremely angular features were set with a prevailing sharpness of expression which defied any unseemly mirth or undue levity in her presence.

"Why, Prudence!" exclaimed Uncle Dan, "is that you?"

"That," said Aunt Prudence, with uncompromising severity of tone, "is me."

" Why — why — where did you come from ? "

"I came," said Aunt Prudence, in the same severe tone of voice, "from the dining-room." "And," she added, before Uncle Dan could ask another question, "if you don't get up and come to breakfast this minute I'll know the reason why."

Uncle Dan slowly clambered to his feet.

" Did you call me, Prudence ? " he said.

"Call you," retorted Aunt Prudence, indignantly, "I should say I did. I called you three times at the top of my voice, and then I rang the bell. But I might as well have tried to wake the dead."

"And what did you do then?"

"Then," said Aunt Prudence, grimly, " I pinched you."

"Oh!" exclaimed Uncle Dan, and without another word followed his excellent wife to the dining-room.

"What you can find interesting to look at every morning out of that window," said Aunt Prudence, as she poured the coffee, "is beyond my comprehension."

" The view," said Uncle Dan, with returning enthusiasm and renewed good nature, "is perfectly delightful."

"Delightful!" retorted Aunt Prudence, with a sniff of disgust, "I should say so. A few old stunted trees and a lot of dirty stables, with dust, dust, dust over everything. Delightful place, indeed!"

Uncle Dan made no reply, but silently buttered his toast, and stirred his coffee as if thus to indicate the entire uselessness of arguing the question with such a prejudiced person as Aunt Prudence.

"And as for the neighbors," continued that worthy lady, "I never did see such a set in all my born days. It's borrow and beg and steal from one another all day long. I declare, 'I haven't a flat-iron left, and where any of my pie-pans are I'm sure I couldn't tell."

"Give to him that asketh thee, and from him that would borrow of thee turn not thou away," said Uncle Dan, softly.

"I never do," said Aunt Prudence, sharply, "and you know I never do, Daniel. I've loaned so many of my kitchen things that there are hardly enough of them left to get dinner with. I don't begrudge them, and you know I don't, Daniel; and I would like to know what you mean by saying that I do."

"Why, I didn't say so, Prudence."

"Yes, you did. You quoted Scripture, and when you quote Scripture you mean something by it."

Uncle Dan looked for a few seconds with a grave and puzzled expression at a little round knob that graced the top of the coffee-pot lid. Conscious of the fact that with the best of intentions it was his unfortunate fate to repeatedly say or do something which brought him into trouble, he regarded the coffee-pot with earnest attention, while he mentally reviewed the scriptural quotation in order to discover, if he might, what there was amiss about it.

Finding nothing in his remark or in his manner with which to reproach himself, and gathering courage from his innocence of any intention to wound the feelings of his worthy spouse, Uncle Dan ventured to look up, and with a broad smile and unruffled good humor, to say, —

"Dear me, Prudence! I don't see how I could possibly quote Scripture without meaning something by it, unless I did it in my sleep. But I meant no reproof, Prudence, not in the least; and I'm sure, my dear, I had no idea of saying anything unpleasant to you."

"That's all very well," retorted Aunt Prudence, "but there is no occasion for quoting Scripture.

As if I don't know what's in the Bible without having it thrown at my head."

"Dear me!" exclaimed Uncle Dan, quite innocently, "I never throw anything at your head, Prudence."

"Very well, then," replied Aunt Prudence, "don't do it. I don't object to lending my things; but I do like to have my neighbors show some appreciation of a favor; and I certainly would like to have them return the things they borrow from me when they are done with them. When I want the stewpan I must run over to Mrs. McGunnegle's for it; and if I want to heat some water or broil a steak I must tramp over to Mrs. Callworthy's or Mrs. Haddick's for the tea-kettle or the broiler, as the case may be. Now I suppose you've got some Scripture at the end of your tongue to show that it's a Christian duty for me to do that."

Aunt Prudence stopped for the double purpose of breathing and of favoring Uncle Dan with a defiant glance. But Uncle Dan, absorbed in the benevolent occupation of rescuing a fly who was in imminent danger of drowning in a glass of water, made no reply. And Aunt Prudence, after having recovered her breath and taken a sip of coffee, went on to say, "It is well enough, Daniel, for you to think that these matters are trifles, and that I ought to put up with them. But when you come to keep house for a week or two you will find how very aggravating they are."

The fly, notwithstanding that it was the object of Uncle Dan's anxiously humane attention, manifested the most singularly obstinate and ungrateful determination to drown in spite of him.

"Dear me!" exclaimed Mr. Poldertot at length, as the fly again slid from the point of his knife into the water, "one would suppose that the poor thing had been disappointed in love. It seems so extremely anxious to commit suicide."

"The fly don't want to drown any more than you do," said Aunt Prudence, with the brusqueness that was characteristic of the lady; "give me that glass."

This request was quite superfluous, since, without awaiting Uncle Dan's compliance with it, the good lady seized the tumbler with her left hand, while at the same moment she elevated a teaspoon with the right, and, plunging the latter into the water, quietly removed the obstinate fly from its perilous position.

"Dear me!" exclaimed Uncle Dan, favoring Aunt Prudence with a generous look of admiration, "that was well done, my dear. Why couldn't I have thought of that?"

With a self-denial that was worthy of a place beside the brightest examples of that sterling virtue, Aunt Prudence forbore from making any comment upon Uncle Dan's clumsiness; and simply contented herself with an expression of disgust, which might have been intended for the fly or for Uncle Dan or for the handle of the coffee-pot, toward which the worthy lady's glance was now directed, or for any two or all of these articles.

As Aunt Prudence evinced no immediate desire to renew the conversation, but simply conveyed her bread to her mouth with her right and her coffee with her left hand alternately, with a mechanical motion that was quite automatic in its silent and clock-like regularity, Uncle Dan felt the necessity (which no one but such a kind, simple-hearted, and good-natured soul would under the same circumstances have felt), of saying something, and accordingly, having first carefully buttered a piece of toast and placed it, ready to be conveyed to his mouth as soon as he should have spoken, directed his smiling face toward his wife, and said, " There was one remark, my dear, which I did not quite understand."

That Aunt Prudence's lips pressed closely together, that her eyes opened, though very slightly, wider, that she just perceptibly shrugged her shoulders and nodded her head, thereby intimating her rather sarcastic belief in the fact which had just been stated, owing to the highly probable circumstance that there were many things which Uncle Dan did not understand, cannot be denied; and that Uncle Dan, although his mild, blue eyes were fixed upon his able helpmate, failed to observe this quiet pantomime is equally beyond dispute; since, in the first place, Uncle Dan's gentle and unsuspecting nature had not yet learnt to note and appreciate those finer shades of sarcasm, which can only be conveyed in the almost imperceptible and indescribable motions of the human features; and, in the second place, Uncle Dan's trusty spectacles were not upon his nose; and when Uncle Dan's spectacles were not upon his nose Uncle Dan's eyes, so far as any sharpness of sight is concerned, were entirely useless. Wherefore, Uncle Dan went on to say, with as much beaming good nature as could possibly shine in his round, broad, ruddy face, " Yes, my dear, there was one remark which I did not quite understand. You spoke just now about the neighbors, and I believe you stated that when I came to keep house for a week or two I would find how very aggravating they are. Dear me! What could you have meant by it? I don't expect to keep house, my love."

"And I," said Aunt Prudence, suddenly opening her mouth and expelling the words as if she were possessed of a sort of vocal pop-gun, "expect you will."

"Ah!" said Uncle Dan, in that gentle tone of incredulity which signifies both unbelief in what has been said and disinclination to contradict the speaker, "and how is that, Prudence?"

"Why," replied Aunt Prudence, "simply, that I am going to the country."

Uncle Dan looked at his estimable lady with eyes that expressed the most unbounded astonishment. The cup which was on its way to his lips descended again to the table, the knife which he had held in his right hand fell upon his plate, and the piece of toast which he had a moment before placed upon the edge of the table, removed by an unvoluntary motion of his hand, tumbled to the floor, butter side down.

"The country!" exclaimed Uncle Dan, at length, "you don't mean to say that ——"

"I am going to the country," said Aunt Prudence, with great distinctness, emphasizing each word with an energetic nod; "that is precisely what I am going to do."

"But — but — but — when are you going, Prudence?" said Uncle Dan.

"This afternoon, at half past three."

"And — dear me! Whom do you expect to visit?"

"Sister Sarah."

"And how do you propose to go?"

"Brother John intends to call for me."

"With his wagon?"

"With his wagon."

"And how long do you expect to stay, Prudence?"

"About two or three weeks."

"Well — well — well — well!"

Uncle Dan's astonishment having exhausted itself in these words left him with nothing further to say. Whereupon he picked up his toast and began to stir his coffee in silence.

"Yes," said Aunt Prudence, unbending from her severe manner to make this explanation, "I received a letter from Brother John, inviting me to spend a few weeks with Sister Sarah. He writes that he will call for me this afternoon. You have no objection to my going, have you, Daniel?"

Aunt Prudence made this last inquiry as if it would not make a particle of difference whether he had any objection or not. Still Uncle Dan replied very warmly, "Not at all — not at all — I am only surprised — a little, — because I had not heard it mentioned before — but it's a capital idea — fresh air, country milk — fruits, flowers, sunshine, plenty of horses, cows, dogs, chickens — delightful, — delightful, — go — go, Prudence, — by all means, go."

"Well, then," observed Aunt Prudence, smartly, "that's settled."

Whereupon the worthy lady arose, and, holding her head as stiffly upright as if her neck was incapable of bending, gathered her apron in her hands and advanced, with a stately step, to the fireplace ; where, permitting the apron to fall, she gravely pretended to brush the crumbs into the fire ; a performance, it is almost needless to say, which was purely unnecessary, since there was neither fire nor grate in the wall nor crumbs in Aunt Prudence's apron, as Uncle Dan or any one acquainted with his good wife's proverbial neatness would cheerfully have testified.

Having carefully disposed of the imaginary crumbs, and smoothed down her apron with both hands, Aunt Prudence turned, and, in the same dignified manner in which she had approached the fireplace, returned toward Uncle Dan and the table ; but she had scarcely advanced half the distance which separated them when she suddenly stopped, a look of doubt, of irresolution, crept into her face, and she exclaimed, "Daniel, look here!"

Uncle Dan, hearing this gentle summons, immediately proceeded to obey it; first gently replacing the cup from which he had been drinking upon the table, then carefully wiping his lips with his napkin, and as carefully spreading the napkin again upon his knees, then softly rubbing the palms of his hands together, then the palm of his right over the back of his left, then the palm of his left over the back of his right, and, just as Aunt Prudence's patience was about exhausted, turned his smiling face toward her, and said, "Well, my dear?"

Aunt Prudence held her elbows close against her side, and lightly pressed the tips of the fingers of her hands together.

"I — I am — a little afraid to ——"

"Afraid to!"

Uncle Dan spoke in a tone of gentle incredulity; as one who doubts the fact stated as he understands it, but is willing to concede that there may be a hidden meaning in the words.

"Afraid to!" — repeated Uncle Dan, after a momentary pause, during which Aunt Prudence appeared to be revolving some weighty question in her mind, — "why, my dear, I have never known you to be afraid in all your life. Afraid to what?"

"Afraid to leave you here alone," said Aunt Prudence.

"And why?"

"Because somebody will impose upon you or rob you or set the house on fire, — or something of the kind."

"Dear me!" exclaimed Uncle Dan, "sufficient unto the day is the evil thereof."

Aunt Prudence separated her fingers with a jerk, and brought her hands together with a sharp little slap.

"Quoting Scripture won't keep away thieves or put out a fire, — and as sure as I go away you will be in danger of both. I don't know what to do about it."

Uncle Dan appeared distressed, and for a moment a cloud rested upon his sunny face. But instantly raising it again, he said, with renewed animation, "Prudence, my dear, I have it."

"Well," said Aunt Prudence.

"We will invite some one to stay here with me while you are gone, — some one in whom we both have confidence. What do you say to that, Prudence?"

"I'll think of it, — I'll think of it," said Aunt

Prudence, in her naturally sharp, decisive tone, — "we will dine at two and we can think it over until then. Mind, sharp two, Daniel. For Brother John is always prompt, and we will have to start early, for we have a long distance to go, and I don't want to ride at night. If you are not here by three o'clock you will not find me."

"Dear me!" said Uncle Dan.

This favorite exclamation was apt to escape from Uncle Dan's lips upon the slightest provocation.

"Yes," continued Aunt Prudence, with a sharp nod; "Three o'clock, — not later. Dinner at two, — to the minute. And now you had better take down a basket and send home something from the market. And don't let anybody impose on you."

And with these words, Aunt Prudence began to bustle round in a state of unrivalled activity. And having, in an incredibly short space of time, bustled Uncle Dan under his hat and into his coat, she placed the basket upon his arm and bustled him out of the house almost before the astonishment awakened by these active proceedings had worn off. And in this abrupt but effective manner was Uncle Dan dispatched upon his daily journey to the haunts of business and the marts of trade.

CHAPTER II.

The distressing occurrences connected with the purchase of vegetables; showing the extraordinary facility possessed by Uncle Dan for getting into trouble; and how he got out of it.

IT was with a heavy heart that Uncle Dan, obedient to the wishes of his energetic lady, proceeded in the direction of the market for the purpose of making the required purchase for the noonday meal.

It was with a heavy heart, we say; for the good woman upon whom Uncle Dan had lavished his unremitting affection for a quarter of a century had become to him, by sheer force of her stronger will and nature, a necessity and a support; and visions of all the dire things that might happen to him or to their pleasant little home during the absence of the guardian angel, as Uncle Dan took pleasure in calling her, appalled him. For, although Uncle Dan had carefully presented a smiling face and spoken in his customary cheery manner when Aunt Prudence announced her intention of leaving him for a short season, doing this in the kindness of his heart that she might have no thought of any annoyance or regret upon his part to detract from the pleasure of her visit, he nevertheless contemplated the coming two or three weeks of loneliness with a species of consternation, and wondered how in the world he could ever manage to worry through it.

But Uncle Dan's nature was of an elastic kind, which refused to be long depressed by any misfortune, however sad or heavy. And so, under the influence of the charming weather and his own comfortable disposition, Uncle Dan soon recovered his good spirits, and began to smile and beam in his usual happy manner upon all around him.

In this pleasant frame of mind Uncle Dan soon approached a long, rectangular brick building, surrounded on all sides by a great number of wooden stalls in two rows — one row occupying the inner and the other the outer edge of the pavement, while in the street, ranged side by side, were long rows of butchers' and country wagons.

These wooden stalls and wagons, appropriated to the disposal and sale of meats, vegetables, fruits, flowers, and a general medley of goods to tempt the eye of the observing passer-by, combined to form, if not a very harmonious, at least a very animated scene; while the narrow pavement between the rows of wooden stalls was crowded with people, who pushed each other, trod on each other's toes, bumped each other with their baskets, and elbowed one another about in that busy, bustling, and not over-gentle manner which is characteristic of humanity in the neighborhood of a crowded market on Saturday morning.

"Dear me!" exclaimed Uncle Dan, as he surveyed the scene through his gold-rimmed spectacles from the opposite side of the street, "what a multitude of people! Where can they all have come from? Where can they all be going to? It looks as if the whole city has come to market this morning. A grand sight! A grand sight! If Prudence were only here!" And having uttered these exclamations, Uncle Dan crossed the street, and, with a light step and a face shining with an excess of good humor, plunged into the midst of the surging crowd, and, in so doing, plunged suddenly and unexpectedly into the midst of trouble. For, being by nature the kindest and gentlest soul in the world, and being of necessity an exceedingly polite and accommodating gentleman, he was prone to give way before everybody, and availed himself of none of those abrupt, rude, and ungentlemanly actions which the people around and about him made use of to push their way along. The consequence was that when Uncle Dan stepped back to make way for a very fat lady and a tremendous basket which filled the path before him, he trod involuntarily upon the tender toes of an old gentleman afflicted with the gout. With an exclamation of pain, the old gentleman inserted the point of a stout ebony cane with extreme violence between Uncle Dan's shoulder-blades, causing that worthy gentleman to spring suddenly forward, knock down a boy with a basket of potatoes, and grasp a lady's arm to keep himself from falling. The lady, thus rudely and unexpectedly surprised in the interesting occupation of purchasing a peck of apples, glanced around in a startled manner, and finding herself thus held by a strange man, uttered a piercing scream and pulled her arm away. Whereupon Uncle Dan staggered heavily against a colored woman with a baby on her arms, who indignantly pushed him against a man with the rheumatism, who, in turn, repelled Uncle Dan so violently that he flew across the pavement and brought up against a candy-stand, the owner of which immediately announced his horrible intention of "spilling him all over the sidewalk."

"I really beg your pardon, sir," said Uncle Dan, " I assure you I couldn't help it — I — "

"Blamed if I don't feel like knocking the whole

top of your head off," growled the man. "Can't you see where you're a-goin' to?"

"An accident, sir, a pure accident."

At this moment Uncle Dan felt his basket pushed violently aside, while an angry voice exclaimed, " Keep your old basket out of people's eyes, will you?"

Uncle Dan in great distress immediately turned around to apologize, whereby the unfortunate basket was brought into sudden contact with the head of a little girl who instantly burst into tears and cried with the whole power of her lungs.

"I wish people would attend to their business and not come here to strike little children," cried a lady who was evidently the child's mother.

"He's a awkward old blunderbuss," said the fat woman who sold sauerkraut.

"He shouldt be knocket on de headt," observed her neighbor with the schmierkase.

"An' it's meself would loike to do it," vindictively observed the man who sold chickens and eggs.

"He ought to be arrested," cried a stout boarding-house lady.

Uncle Dan was in perfect misery. He stood quite still, with the perspiration starting out on his round, ruddy face, with every appearance of helpless consternation, afraid to move in any direction lest he should innocently commit some other fearful trespass upon the rights or feelings of the people around him, and wishing in his heart of hearts that he was a thousand miles away, and that Aunt Prudence stood in his place.

While Uncle Dan stood in this predicament, staring pitifully from one to another of the angry faces around him, a person who had heard the commotion in the distance began to push and elbow his way through the crowd toward the spot where Uncle Dan was standing. This person was a tall, broad-shouldered young man, with a smooth face, hair cut very short, and a particularly bright pair of sharp, gray eyes. A certain ease and freedom with which this young gentleman made his way through the crowd, unceremoniously inserting his broad shoulders between the people and pushing them aside, making way with his elbows where his shoulders were too large, without much care as to whose ribs they came in contact with, and paying no attention whatever to the snarls and growls of the people around him, justified the conclusion that he was a young gentleman who was abundantly able to take care of himself under any circumstances whatever. And yet there was in his whole bearing a something which suggested an inclination to take things easy in this world, which sometimes amounted to an expression of positive indolence; as if the question whether there was anything in this life worth striving for was still in process of debate, and until that point was settled there was no necessity for taking more than a passing interest in anything that might transpire.

This young gentleman, coming suddenly before Uncle Dan at the moment that that harassed individual was revolving a wild project in his mind concerning a bold dash for liberty, right over the sauerkraut bucket, around the candy-stand, through the market-house, over the fish-tank, and thence goodness knows where, caused Mr. Poldertot to exclaim, in accents of mingled relief and astonishment, "Why, Dick! My dear boy, is that you? I am glad to see you, Dick, very glad to see you."

Dick, or as he may here be properly introduced, Mr. Richard Doolittle, inclined his head slightly in acknowledgment of this hearty greeting, and suffered Uncle Dan to grasp his hand and shake it.

"You see, Dick," continued Uncle Dan, "I have unfortunately got myself into a peck of trouble."

"Bushels," laconically remarked Mr. Doolittle, glancing complacently around at the angry faces.

Uncle Dan opened his mouth to reply, but was immediately overwhelmed by an indignant chorus from the various produce venders and others, including an india-rubber balloon man and an orange peddler, who had just come upon the scene and knew nothing about the affair; but who evidently deemed it good policy to shout, like Mr. Pickwick, with the crowd.

How long the chorus continued or how loud it became is immaterial, since immediately upon the first outburst Mr. Doolittle calmly linked arms with Uncle Dan, and uttering the two simple but highly expressive monosyllables, "Oh, bosh!" actually pushed his elderly friend through the crowd, which was rapidly increasing in size.

"Dick," said Uncle Dan, when they had reached a comparatively open spot at the end of the market, "I am a thousand times obliged to you, my boy. I don't know what I should have done without you, Dick." And, in an excess of gratitude, Mr. Poldertot shook Dick's right hand with both of his own.

"Pshaw!" said Dick, relapsing into indolence again, "that's nothing. Don't trouble about it. Let's take it easy."

"I can't help it, Dick. You have done me a great favor and I won't forget it," replied Uncle Dan, still overflowing with the gratitude which beamed in his ruddy face and shone through his spectacles from his mild blue eyes.

But suddenly a look of grave concern overspread his face, and he broke into his customary ejaculation of "Dear me! Dear me!"

Mr. Doolittle simply elevated his eyebrows in an almost imperceptible manner; and with no other sign or word gave the slightest intimation that he had heard Uncle Dan's remark, or, if he had, that he had the slightest interest in the circumstance which had occasioned it.

"You see," spoke Mr. Poldertot further, with slight pauses between his words as if to note their effect upon his apparently disinterested listener, "you see — you know — I am sent — Aunt Prudence ——"

Mr. Doolittle shut one eye very tight, puckered his mouth, put his hands into his pockets, and looked down at Uncle Dan with a comical expression of attention.

Uncle Dan evidently understood him, for he continued as if his friend had made audible reply.

"Yes — so she is — a little sharp — a little — not irritable; no, she is never that, but — ah —

touchy sometimes — still, nevertheless, — the best woman in the world, Dick; the best woman in the world."

Dick opened the eye that was closed and closed the eye that was open and said nothing.

Taking one of the buttons of Mr. Doolittle's coat between the thumb and forefinger of his right hand, and examining it closely as if it was an intricate piece of machinery which required the keenest scrutiny and the most careful study to be properly appreciated and understood, Uncle Dan went on to say, still hesitatingly as before, " Nevertheless, Dick — although she is the finest woman in the world — which nobody can deny — I must acknowledge that she is a little particular about her household arrangements; and when she says to me, 'send home something from the market,' I rather think that she will be — a trifle — disappointed unless she gets the things in good season — and plenty of them. You understand me, Dick ?"

Dick's mouth puckered until there was nothing left of it but a small orifice surrounded by wrinkles, both of his eyes were firmly closed for the space of a few seconds, succeeded by the opening of the one which had been last closed, and then his head was gravely inclined toward Uncle Dan. And it may safely be concluded that by all this pantomimic action Dick intended to make known that Uncle Dan's meaning was, thus far, perfectly clear, and that he was prepared to give strict attention to what Mr. Poldertot might still have to say.

So, at least, Uncle Dan understood him, and thereupon he continued, still feeling Dick's button with the greatest care, "Yes, you see, she likes good meats and vegetables and an abundance of them — not that I mean to say that she likes them on her own account, Dick," Uncle Dan hastened to add, fearful that his words might have created a wrong impression.

Dick solemnly shook his head, whereupon Uncle Dan went on, "She usually does the marketing herself — and she always astonishes me with the variety of articles she gets — and so cheap, too! (She's very economical, you know, Dick.) Now I am certain that if I venture into that crowd again they will take some advantage of me. It's really astonishing how much worthless stuff some of these people do impose on me. And as for charges! Why, Dick, to tell you the truth, Prudence can buy twice as much as I can for the same money. And what I am to do about it, dear me! I really cannot tell."

"Here," said Dick, suddenly opening his eyes

very wide, "I'll arrange it — I know what Aunt Prudence wants. I'll buy it," and with these words Dick took the basket from Uncle Dan's arm before that gentleman quite understood what his young friend meant.

"Dear me! Dear me! Will you do that? Well, now, that is real kind of you, Dick. But I am afraid it will take too much of your time."

"Nothing to do," said Dick, "folks all gone east — left me to watch the house and keep bachelor's hall."

"Dear me! and why didn't I think of it before? Why, Dick, I am in the same predicament. I, too, must keep bachelor's hall."

"How?" inquired Dick, shortly.

"Why, you see, Dick, Prudence is going to visit her sister, and so I shall be left alone for a week or two. Rather lonesome — don't you think so?"

Dick nodded.

Uncle Dan looked gloomily at Dick for several moments; but suddenly his face brightened and he clapped his hands together in an ecstasy of joy.

"Dear me! I have it! We can room together. You can lodge with me. Just the thing — and that will suit Prudence, I know. And we'll have a splendid time, Dick, a splendid time!"

"Aunt Prudence —" began Dick.

"Prudence wishes it," said Uncle Dan, quickly. "The only thing that mars her enjoyment is the thought that I shall be left alone. Excellent, considerate woman! Will you come, Dick? Is it agreed?"

"Done," said Dick. And then Mr. Doolittle turned, and plunging into the crowd was soon lost to sight.

"Dear me! Dear me!" said Uncle Dan, as he crossed the street, with a face that was radiant with happiness and good nature, "what a splendid young fellow he is, to be sure! Always ready to help a person in trouble," and having thus spoken (unconsciously aloud, much to the astonishment of a number of ladies who were passing at the time), Uncle Dan hurried on, without further delay, to his place of business, a little queensware and crockery store on Franklin avenue.

CHAPTER III.

Which, besides containing a description of Mr. Poldertot's establishment, embraces the record of the marvellous disappearance of a suit of clothes, and finally tells what became of it.

THE establishment toward which Uncle Dan had directed his steps, and upon the profits of which he depended for a modest livelihood, was distinguished by an imposing array of empty cups and saucers in a basket at the door, a long plank suspended on a nail against the wall, and embellished with a row of plates grown dingy through long exposure to the weather, a china bulldog with a viciously impudent stare on his green, stony countenance, a number of squatty red, white and blue coal-oil lamps seductively inscribed with the legend, "ONLY ONE DOLLAR," and a weather-stained old sign above the door which gave the world to understand (in faded red letters on a soiled white background) that the business below, represented by the aforesaid cups, saucers, bulldog and coal-oil lamps, was conducted under the firm name of DANIEL POLDERTOT & CO.

The remotest records in the possession of Uncle Dan failed to show who the company of the concern was, or ever had been. And as no one had ever been known to see anybody in the store who pretended to exercise any proprietary right, (with the exception of Uncle Dan and Aunt Prudence,) it may be safe to infer that the addition of "& Co." to the firm name was simply a pleasant fiction invented to make an impression upon the public, or to bother the tax collector. And as I am certain that Uncle Dan was entirely too kind-hearted to give intentional trouble to even his worst enemy, we must reject the latter view and come to the conclusion that the sole purpose for which the name of the firm was extended beyond the simple name of the proprietor, was to create a favorable impression upon the mind of the general public. In doing which Uncle Dan simply followed an old and honorable precedent which the respected reader has probably noticed in his or her own city — namely; the application of a tremendously long name to an exceedingly small business.

When Uncle Dan finally reached his store and entered it, the first sight that greeted him was a boy, clad in a pair of extremely ragged trousers, a gray woollen shirt, and one suspender, who was busily engaged in the interesting pastime of swinging a kitten by the tail in such a manner that the forepaws hung within an inch of the floor, which it made the most desperate and unavailing efforts to reach.

Uncle Dan's face flushed in an instant. No unprovoked assault upon himself, no inexcusable insult or unnecessary inconvenience thrust upon him, could so bring the light of anger to the mild blue eyes of Mr. Poldertot as the commonplace amusement of teasing a cat. I am positively convinced that if the boy had taken a stick and begun to break all the chinaware with it, including the terrible and ferocious bull-dog, Uncle Dan would not have resented it more.

"Jimmy," said Uncle Dan, in as stern a voice as that soft-hearted gentleman could command, "let that kitten go!"

Jimmy, saluted in this unexpected manner, turned round with marvellous celerity, and presented a face decorated with a pug nose, two small round eyes, a remarkably large mouth, and an unlimited quantity of dirt, while the kitten, released as soon as Uncle Dan's voice was heard, made use of its liberty to dart into an impenetrable labyrinth of mugs, jugs, and pitchers at the other end of the store.

"Jimmy," said Uncle Dan, in a tone of mingled displeasure and reproach, "what do you mean?" Jimmy pulled his suspender and looked up; then he pulled his suspender and looked down; then he put his hands into his pockets and looked around; and, deriving no relief from these performances, he hung his head with the air of a culprit detected in crime, and began rubbing the end of his great toe upon the floor, as if determined to bore a hole through which to disappear from the sight of Uncle Dan forever.

"I don't wonder you have nothing to say," said Uncle Dan; "I am surprised at such conduct."

"Well," said Jimmy, industriously rubbing the floor harder than ever, "that there cat was a scratching the paint o' your desk."

"That does not justify you at all, Jimmy, in practising cruelty to a dumb animal," said Uncle Dan. "The defenceless creatures which a good Providence has generously placed under our protection are dependent upon us for kindness and consideration, and if we violate our trust by torturing them in any way we prove ourselves to be wicked and ungrateful beings; mind that, my boy — wicked and ungrateful beings."

"That there cat," said Jimmy, determined to justify himself, if possible, "was a goin' fur the c'nary bird — an' he knocked down the cage, an' he made a jump fur that there c'nary bird, an' he put his paws in through the wires an' he just grabbed holt of ——"

"Not the canary, Jimmy, not the canary — don't say that!" cried Uncle Dan in the greatest alarm.

"No, sir; the little ring what the bird swings hisself on."

"Dear me! dear me! and what happened then, Jimmy?"

"Then I grabbed a holt o' the cat."

"My brave boy," exclaimed Uncle Dan, a broad smile of gratification immediately illuminating his features, "that was an excellent action upon your part — an excellent action; and I am highly gratified. That does not exactly justify you in swinging the cat by the tail, because you see the cat only followed its natural instincts; but, still, I am exceedingly obliged to you, my boy, for saving the poor little canary; I am, indeed." And Uncle Dan patted the hero kindly on the shoulder.

"But, dear me!" he exclaimed suddenly, holding the hero off at arms-length, "what — what — what has become of your clothes?"

The hero immediately changed into a culprit again, and began boring away on the floor harder than ever.

"Are those the same old clothes you used to wear?"

"Yes'r."

"And didn't I tell you that those clothes were not fit to be seen on a young gentleman in a store?"

"Yes'r."

"And did I not give you a suit of new clothes yesterday afternoon, and made you put it right on?"

"Yes'r."

"Then, Jimmy, what have you done with the new clothes?"

"Nothing."

"Then where are they?"

"I don't know, s'r."

The subject was getting too deep, and so, before proceeding with the next question, Uncle Dan took the liberty of putting on his spectacles; and then, after having favored the objectionable attire with a long, puzzled stare, Uncle Dan continued:

"You have done nothing with the new clothes, and you don't know where they are; now, tell me, who did you give them to? — don't be afraid — speak right out — and tell the truth. Who did you give the garments to, Jimmy?"

"Nobody, s'r."

"Extraordinary!" exclaimed Uncle Dan, "extraordinary!"

"Them there clothes was tuk away, s'r," the culprit ventured to say at last.

"Dear me! dear me! Why, I might have thought of that," said Uncle Dan, with a glance of sympathy, "and so they were stolen, were they?"

The boy hesitated a little and at last said, "No, s'r."

"Extraordinary!" exclaimed Uncle Dan, with increased astonishment, "the clothes were taken and not stolen! Taken without your consent?"

"Yes'r."

"And not stolen?"

"No, s'r."

"Ex-tra-or-di-na-ry!" cried Uncle Dan for the third time. The puzzle was so very deep that the spectacles were of no use whatever; wherefore Uncle Dan pushed them up out of the way; and so they lay on the top of his head blinking at the ceiling.

"Then who in the world," said Uncle Dan, "could have taken them?"

The grimy-faced culprit began to bore his eyes with his knuckles, as he had bored the floor with his toe, in evident distress. Seeing which, Uncle

Dan placed his broad, chubby hand lightly upon the boy's tangled hair and repeated, very kindly, —

"Who could have taken them, my boy?"

"Pap, s'r."

The boring process was increasing in violence.

"Dear me! Your father! And what did he do with them?"

"Sold 'em, s'r."

The knuckles were twirled harder still.

"Sold them, Jimmy! What for?"

"Whiskey, s'r."

And then both hands began to bore with all their might, and the dirty culprit-hero burst into tears.

CHAPTER IV.

Introducing two great geniuses (although as yet unknown to fame) who are destined to frequently reappear in these pages. — A perplexity. — A bright idea.

IT is quite uncertain into what extravagant expression of sympathy Uncle Dan was preparing to launch — for the sight of tears always stirred his gentle heart to its lowest depths — as at this moment there entered two young gentlemen, who approached smilingly and cried simultaneously, —

"Uncle Dan, how do you do?"

Uncle Dan hastily pulled down the spectacles from the top of his head and placed them on the end of his nose, — for what earthly reason it is impossible to say, since he deliberately looked right over them. He had no sooner done this than he advanced with outstretched hands and a cheerful smile of welcome, while he said, —

"Bob! Harry! Dear me! dear me! I'm glad to see you, my young friends, I'm glad to see you. Why, I'm — I'm *delighted* to see you."

The two young gentlemen with whom Uncle Dan was at this moment shaking hands with every evidence of pleasure were a very short little gentleman, with a remarkably large head and a crop of bushy, light-brown hair, and a medium-sized young gentleman, with a pair of pale-blue eyes and a high forehead, whom it is the narrator's pleasure to introduce respectively as Mr. Robert Sturdy and Mr. Harry Cribbler.

"Uncle Dan," said Mr. Robert Sturdy, "we have come to ask a favor of you."

"And we hope you will grant it," said the other gentleman, who was Mr. Harry Cribbler.

"Hope he will! I should say so! Of course he will; no doubt about it," retorted Mr. Sturdy, with an air of great positiveness.

"My dear young friends," said Uncle Dan, still smiling, and still shaking hands as if he was a patent machine made especially for the purpose and had been wound up to run all day, "any favor which I can grant is, as you very well know, granted already."

Mr. Cribbler looked pleased and relieved, as if he had expected to be disappointed.

Mr. Sturdy looked pleased and positive, as if he nad expected nothing else.

"Certainly, certainly," continued Uncle Dan,

"you may depend upon it. What can I do for you, my boys?"

"Now," said Mr. Sturdy, speaking with a curious appearance of knowing all the time that somebody intended to contradict him, and that he was not going to submit to it, "I'll tell you what it is, Uncle Dan — and it's only this — Harry and Dick Doolittle and myself intend making a visit to Milton, say next week or week after next. Now, I don't care who says we've not quite decided about it yet — I say we have — and we're going. You see I'm tired of painting, Harry he's tired of writing, and Dick's tired of doing nothing. So we're going to have a vacation to take some of the rust off."

"An excellent idea, Bob, an excellent idea," said Uncle Dan, heartily.

"Of course it's an excellent idea," said Bob. "I'd like to hear anybody deny it."

"And so we thought — " began Mr. Cribbler.

"Now, you hold on," said Bob, elevating his forefinger and pointing it at Mr. Cribbler as if it was a loaded pistol, "*you* hold on. Wait till *I'm* through, and then *you* begin."

It was a comical sight — this abrupt way in which little Bob disposed of his friends; as if they were the veriest pigmies and he a giant at least ten feet high.

"So you see, Uncle Dan, we intend to have a good time. But we need assistance, because, you know, Dick's a little sleepy, I'm a little heavy, and Harry here's a little soft. Yes, you are, and you needn't deny it."

Mr. Cribbler had not uttered a word, and when Mr. Sturdy pounced upon him in this manner he only smiled and nodded pleasantly at Uncle Dan, who also smiled and nodded pleasantly at him, as if they understood each other and Mr. Sturdy very well, as no doubt they did.

"What we want," said Bob, "is somebody to go with us who can keep us straight and help us have a good time. Now, who do you think that is, Uncle Dan?"

"I'm sure I can't tell," said Uncle Dan.

"That," said Bob, elevating his forefinger and pointing it at Uncle Dan, "is you."

"I!" said Uncle Dan.

"You," repeated Bob.

"You," seconded Harry.

"Well — well — I — dear me! dear me!"

"Yes," continued Harry, "and that is the favor we intended to ask of you. The trip will do you good, I know, and we will be ever so much obliged to you if you will go. Now, you will, Uncle Dan, won't you?"

"Of course he will," exclaimed Bob. "The thing's settled. What's the use of talking about it?"

"But — but — my dear boys," began Uncle Dan, at length, "I really——"

"No buts, Uncle Dan, no buts," said Bob.

"Bob, I should be delighted to go with you, but it is impossible. I really cannot leave the store. Jimmy is not quite old enough to be left in charge of the business, although I must say that he is beginning to show decided signs of improvement."

Bob and Harry looked at Jimmy rather dubiously, as if the only signs they could discover about him just at that moment were signs of dirt.

"Why don't you," said Bob, levelling the loaded pistol again, "hire a clerk?"

"Just what I have been thinking for some time — but you see the business can't afford a very high-priced man, and as to finding a trustworthy man who is willing to work for a very small salary, I am sure I shouldn't know where to look for one."

"Lots of them laying around," said Bob, curtly, "lots of them."

As if they were a species of vegetables or wild fruit that might be had for the picking.

"Can you not find a suitable person by inquiring among your friends?" persuasively suggested Mr. Cribbler.

"Of course he can, or by putting a notice in the window," asserted Mr. Sturdy.

"You see," continued Mr. Cribbler, "you never know what you can do till you try. And possibly you could find a gentleman or a lady who would be glad to accept the situation and work faithfully in it even for a moderate salary."

Uncle Dan's face suddenly lighted up, and, while he rubbed his hands in token of extreme satisfaction, he said, "Dear me! why didn't I think of it before? Why, my dear boys, I'll — I'll ADVERTISE!" And Mr. Poldertot expelled this word as triumphantly as if it were the key to all the riddles that have perplexed the earth from the very beginning.

"Capital!" cried Harry and Bob together, "just the thing!"

Uncle Dan's happy idea having thus met with unanimous approval not a moment was lost in acting upon it.

Two or three sheets of foolscap were immediately spread out upon a small shaky desk, pens and ink were ceremoniously placed in position, Uncle

Dan took his seat before the desk, picked up one of the pens, dipped it in the ink, carefully tried the nib on his thumb-nail and began to write.

But even an advertisement cannot be written without a moment's thought. And so, after the pen had traced the talismanic words " Wanted," it came to a dead stop, and Uncle Dan looked up at the ceiling like a distracted poet who cannot find suitable words that will rhyme.

At length with the help of Mr. Cribbler and Mr. Sturdy, who stood behind Uncle Dan and looked over his shoulder, the following composition was produced, —

> WANTED. — A thoroughly trustworthy lady or gentleman, who is willing to accept a small salary, to act as general assistant and salesman in a queensware store. One who has some knowledge of keeping books preferred.
>
> D. POLDERTOT, 1159 Franklin Avenue.

" And now," said Bob, " we must go."

" Don't hurry; stay a few moments," said Uncle Dan.

" No," said Bob, " can't stay another minute — just began Napoleon — life size — grand affair; going to make a thousand-dollar picture of it. I've got the conception right here " — Mr. Sturdy lightly tapped his prominent forehead to show where he had it, — " and must get to work before the inspiration passes away. Harry's got to the seventeenth chapter of the third volume of his

Great American Novel — it's a fine thing, I tell you — good ways ahead of any of those trashy English things — going to make him famous, it is. I read one chapter — beautiful! He'll lend you the first volume, Uncle Dan. You'll like it. It's better than Dickens or Thackeray or any of the rest of 'em. Yes, it is, Harry, and you needn't stand there shaking your head. When I see a good thing I know it. So come on and don't stand talking there all day. We've got some work to do. Good bye, Uncle Dan. Don't forget — Milton, Tuesday week," and, so speaking, the great artist (as yet unknown to fame) linked arms with the wonderful writer (also as yet unknown to fame), and left Uncle Dan deep in the perplexing problem of how much he could afford to pay for the services of an assistant.

The unyielding necessities of truth compel us to admit that the two incipient great men had only proceeded half a square from Uncle Dan's house when they overtook two charming young ladies. And as the said charming young ladies smilingly invited them to play a game of croquet, and as the day was beautiful and the ladies irresistible, the invitation was accepted. Wherefore the great Napoleon remained upon his easel and the Great American Novel in its desk, in dark and undisturbed seclusion.

CHAPTER V.

A mysterious communication, which causes a noble resolution to animate the heart of Uncle Dan.

AUNT Prudence had departed and Dick had not yet come, when at precisely ten minutes of nine o'clock P. M., Uncle Dan stood upon the pavement before his store-door, nervously feeling his plain black watchguard and watching the twinkling gas lights that stretched far away in the distance upon both sides of the street. As he stood thus absent-mindedly permitting his eye to travel from one flaring gas jet to the other, his face wore a look expressive of the deepest misery and gloom. The remembrance of Aunt Prudence's departure still lay heavily upon his heart. And in a most dejected manner Uncle Dan stood there revolving the whole matter in his mind and becoming more and more miserable every moment that he did so.

So pre-occupied was Uncle Dan with these regretful thoughts that he paid no attention what ever to the stream of people which was passing and repassing; and he would in all probability have stood there a long time without noticing a single man, woman or child, had there not appeared at this moment two figures who advanced from the opposite side of the street and halted within three feet of Uncle Dan. Even then Uncle Dan did not recognize them until a familiar voice cried, " Uncle Dan, what's the matter?"

"Dear me!" exclaimed Uncle Dan, "dear me! Can that be Dick? It *is* Dick — and Harry. Dear me, where did you come from? Where is Bob?"

When Uncle Dan asked these questions Dick thrust his left hand into his pocket, shook hands with Uncle Dan with his right, half shut his eyes, formed a tube of his mouth as if with the intention of whistling, thought better of it, allowed his mouth to relax, and then shrugged his shoulders and shook his head with an appearance of the profoundest mystery; thereby indicating the possession of some strange and interesting secret in relation to his friend Bob which would astonish and overwhelm Uncle Dan as soon as he heard it.

Harry, more frank and open than Dick, immediately spoke, but only to such effect that his words confirmed the existence of a mystery hinted at in Dick's actions, and had the effect of plunging Uncle Dan into a state of wondering silence.

"Where is Bob, did you say, Uncle Dan? Well, that's just it; that's just what we want to find out. Where *is* Bob, sure enough?"

"And echo," exclaimed Dick, gravely, "answers, where?"

Dire thoughts of all the likely and unlikely things that could have happened immediately flashed through Uncle Dan's mind. Murder, suicide, highway robbery, abduction, accidental death, instantaneously forced themselves upon his excited imagination, which, to its credit be it said, it promptly rejected as ideas altogether improbable and unworthy of a moment's notice.

"Well, then," said Uncle Dan, in conclusion of these reflections and evidently laboring under the impression that he had audibly expressed them all, "if he has met with no misfortune, where in the world *can* our friend Bob have gone to?"

At this question there passed over Dick's face such a peculiar expression that both Uncle Dan and his friend Harry watched him with amazement. The expression was a smile, and yet it was not a smile. It was a dim illumination as of a light shining through a dirty window, suggesting wonderful possibilities of splendor if only the window were raised; a contraction of the muscles into innumerable wrinkles about the half-open mouth and the half-closed eyes, revelling in mystery, hinting at a secret which was capable of producing an effect not to be excelled by the explosion of a bomb-shell in a company of ladies.

When at last the illumination began to fade as if the light were being diminished or the window becoming dirtier, Uncle Dan ventured to inquire, "Do you know anything about Bob, Dick?"

Dick made no reply, but went through the singular pantomime of turning himself around quickly three times on his left heel, and whistling a stave of "When Johnnie comes marching home again," a ditty which was quite popular during the late civil war.

"Well, can *you* tell me anything, Harry? Dick's tongue seems to be sealed."

"All I can tell you, Uncle Dan," said Harry, "can be told in very few words; and I am afraid they throw very little light upon the subject of Bob's whereabouts. After we left you this morning we met two young ladies and accompanied them home. They invited us to dine with them and we did so; and we then remained in their company until nearly six o'clock. When we left them I went immediately homeward, but Bob said he would call at the office of the paper and leave your advertisement for insertion in to-morrow's issue. Before leaving me he promised to take tea with me at my house at seven o'clock precisely. Now here is the mystery.— He did not come!"

"He did not come!" echoed Uncle Dan.

"He did not come," repeated Harry. "Still, I should not have thought this so very strange if he had not sent me this message," and with these words Harry produced a small folded piece of paper which he handed to Uncle Dan. Uncle Dan took a small leathern case from his vest pocket, and from this drew his spectacles, which he placed, in a most comical manner, upon the very tip end of his nose, and holding the paper so that the light from his store window could fall upon it, began to read Bob's message, which was as follows :—

"DEAR HARRY :—

"I am obliged to disappoint you. Please excuse me, as I have a previous engagement which I am very anxious to keep; and the tea can wait until some other time. Now don't deny it and feel bad about it, because it can, and I'm coming sure some other evening. If Dick says anything— kick him. Kick him anyhow—he deserves it.

"Seriously, Harry, I am going to do something to-night — that is, try to do something which I have intended to do for a long time, and have never had the courage — because you see, it will either make or ruin me for life. It is a serious piece of business, and I feel cold when I think of it. *But the experiment must be made.* If I succeed, you shall know all about it to-morrow. If I fail, and you should ever see me again (which is not likely), I beg of you, old fellow, as a friend upon whom I can rely, never to ask me any questions. Ruined, as I will be, let the secret remain my own, forever.

"Yours truly,
"Robert Sturdy."

Uncle Dan read this remarkable document through to the end, and paled as he did so. At its close he lowered his spectacles and looked over them at Harry in speechless amazement; then he raised the spectacles and looked from under them at Dick in the same silent surprise; then he looked through them at the paper once more, and, finding no enlightenment in these performances, he groaned and said, in a voice of deep sorrow and apprehension, "Dear me! Dear me!"

"What's the matter, Uncle Dan?" said Dick.

Uncle Dan silently handed him the letter and gravely shook his head.

Dick carefully read the letter (with as much apparent interest as if it had not already been shown to him by Harry only a few minutes before), muttered "much obliged," when he came to the complimentary allusion to himself, and having finished it, returned the missive to Uncle Dan with an elaborate show of politeness.

"We must find him," said Uncle Dan, earnestly, "we must find him, Dick, immediately."

"Precisely," assented Harry, "we must learn where he has gone to."

"And what he intends to do. And save him," continued Uncle Dan, "from the danger to which he alludes."

At these words Dick looked gratefully at Uncle Dan and nodded his head; then he looked mysterious and shook his head; then he looked doubtful and shrugged his shoulders; and then he looked determined and said, "I'll try it."

Uncle Dan glanced inquiringly at his young friend, who condescended to explain by saying, "I know where he is."

Uncle Dan looked immensely relieved and said, "Then you must know something about his plans."

Dick nodded his head.

"What is the secret, Dick?"

But to this question Dick would give no direct reply. Only saying, while he looked very sober and mysterious, that he had purposely come to invite Uncle Dan to go with him in order, if possible, to prevent Bob from doing something which he had known him to have in contemplation for a long time, from which he had endeavored to dissuade him but without avail, something which was very serious, and which he could only look upon as being a grave mistake, with, possibly, sad and heart-rending consequences, the success in which enterprise was a thing of (to his mind) very doubtful satisfaction (although, of course, Bob thought otherwise), and the failure in which might lead, as it frequently did, to some great catastrophe.

Speaking in this strain, with many peculiar nods and winks and shrugs, Dick so excited Uncle Dan that that benevolent gentleman determined to accompany him forthwith and endeavor at all hazards to prevent Bob from committing the unknown rash action, or, if too late, at least try to save him from the evil consequences of it.

In a very few moments Uncle Dan's store was closed for the night, a full hour before the usual time, and the three friends were on their way to the scene of Bob's experiment.

And the " blues" which had afflicted Uncle Dan all the afternoon were compelled to give way before the greater anxiety which he now felt for the safety of the valiant Mr. Sturdy.

"Dear me!" exclaimed Uncle Dan, "let us hasten along as fast as we can."

The three companions quickened their pace and lost no time in idle conversation.

And in emulation of this illustrious example, the busy chronicler will lose no time in idle dissertation, but will proceed, with no unnecessary delay, to record in the succeeding chapter the further adventures of Uncle Dan and his three young friends.

CHAPTER VI.

A peculiar street and the peculiar transactions which took place upon it, including the peculiar actions of a peculiar sign.

N the meantime, upon this self-same evening, the moon, shedding its accustomed silvery light indiscriminately over the now shadowy city, devoted a portion of its gentle rays to the illumination of a street in the North End. If appearances were to be trusted, this street had evidently had a hard time of it. For, not only was it in a chronic state of bad repair, not only did it rise obscurely from the sands and backwater of the Mississippi, and, gradually improving as it entered the city, stop ignominiously before some old frame shanties just as it was fairly underway, but, judging from the character of the houses bordering upon it, it existed in a continual state of suspense and warfare with itself between a commendable desire to become a street of note and a natural tendency to go to the dogs.

The result of this struggle was a curious division of the street against itself, making it, as it were, an epitome of the whole city. For, while upon one side it was lined with rows of comfortable dwellings, upon the other side it was supplied with small two-story houses, approached by wooden steps; groceries, surrounded by the usual array of sacks of salt and coal-oil barrels; open lots, always covered more or less with time-worn drays and old spring-wagons; a carpenter-shop; a shoe-shop; and a sickly-looking drug-store, which seemed to be continually in need of its own medicine.

Half-way between the beginning and the end of this street, and upon its common side, stood a short row of two-story brick buildings.

Of these buildings the centre house was rendered conspicuous by the presence of a rusty iron rod fastened in the wall just above the hall door, and extending directly and horizontally over a flight of wooden steps. Very few people who passed that way failed to notice the rusty iron rod, since from it hung suspended a much-battered and time-worn tin sign, which bore the important information (in flaring yellow letters upon a background of black paint),—

"Prof. Claudius Bulbous,
Musician.
Music furnished for balls and parties,"

and which creaked and squeaked dismally in the slightest breeze.

Under this time-honored sign, upon the wooden steps, sat a young lady and a young gentleman engaged in a conversation of such importance that they found it necessary to speak in whispers; which so incensed the old tin sign as being a breach of confidence and a suggestion that it could not be trusted, that it twirled violently around upon its rusty axle, and uttered the most doleful, piercing, and heart-rending sounds; occasionally pausing a moment as if to listen; and then, as if becoming disgusted at its inability to hear a single word, going on again in its reckless revolutions wilder than before.

Ah, if the old tin sign could have heard the whispered conversation! How it would have spun around! How it would have squeaked and moaned and made all sorts of ear-piercing protests against the parties under it, and the subject of their mysterious deliberations. How it would have creaked and ground out a medley of keen metallic flourishes, whose nerve-rasping intonations might thus be interpreted: —

"Professor Bulbous! Professor Bulbous! Your daughter is hatching treason against you, Professor! Take care! Treason, sir, treason! Of the rankest, direst, and most ungrateful kind! Treason! *treason!!* TREASON!!!" until having,

MR. STURDY TRIES TO EXPRESS HIS FEELINGS. — Page 68.

in its choleric swinging, pushed out the little nail which held it confined upon the iron rod, it flew off in a tangent and hid itself in rage and anger in the first dark corner to which the wind would carry it.

"And would you believe," said the young lady, when the conversation had been carried on for some time, "he is coming soon to get an answer."

"Villain!" whispered the young man.

From every appearance this forcible epithet was applied to the solitary individual who dwells in the moon, since the young gentleman glared vindictively in that direction when he spoke, which so abashed the poor moon that it immediately slipped behind a passing cloud. Whereupon there immediately occurred a peculiar explosion under the old tin sign, immediately followed by more angry creaks and dismal wails from that excitable and much-abused object.

The moon, at last, picking up sufficient courage to come slowly out from behind the cloud and peep down at the irate young gentleman, found that individual surprisingly composed, examining, with an air of the most eager attention, a ribbon which was attached to the young lady's hair.

"And what is more," said the young lady, pronouncing her words in an unusually sharp, curt tone, as if she desired to use no more time in the utterance of a word than was absolutely necessary, "my father insists upon my giving him a favorable reception. He wants me to marry him."

"The wretch!"

"Oh, don't call my father that!"

"I did not mean your father, Bella. I meant *him*, the scoundrel!"

And at this juncture the young gentleman looked upward with such a belligerent gaze, at the same time pulling up his sleeves, clenching his fists and shaking his head, that the man in the moon, thoroughly frightened by these warlike demonstrations, scampered behind a very black cloud as fast as he could, and left the scene in total darkness. And during its continuance there occurred such a series of explosions that the weather-beaten sign was rendered crazy with rage and jealousy, and, in its frantic efforts to escape, occasioned the most exquisitely excruciating and discordant music that can ever be imagined.

"And to think," said the young lady, notwithstanding an occasional interruption by one of those singular explosions, "that he should have had the audacity to send me a ring and ask me to wear it on the forefinger of my left hand!"

"Outrageous!" commented the young man, with

as much force as could be compressed within the limits of a whisper.

There can be no doubt that if the miserable and unnamed "him" had been at that moment present something very terrible would have happened. For the young gentleman, finding words inadequate to express his feelings, finished his sentence in pantomime by revolving his clenched fists rapidly around each other, as if these aggressive members had been suddenly transformed into a circular saw, a sight at which the moon, just peeping from behind the dark, black cloud, was so astonished that it sallied forth in full view along the deep blue sky, and looked blandly down upon the interesting scene with a bright glance of wonder and concern.

"And I, really," said the sharp-spoken young lady, "don't know what to do."

"Do you like him at all?"

"You know I don't. I wish he would never come near me."

This answer appeared to be excessively gratifying to the young man; for he toyed gently with the lady's hand and looked upward at the man in the moon with a benignant smile—a favor for which, I have no doubt, that personage was extremely grateful.

"Then, why don't you tell him so?" said the young gentleman.

"Because," rejoined the young lady, uttering the words as if she were snapping their heads off, "because father likes him. When father likes a person, I haven't anything to say. If I should tell that man that I don't like him — oh, my!"

Measureless possibilities of awful things were compressed into this exclamation.

"Why don't you write to him?" suggested the young gentleman.

The lady shook her head vigorously — indeed so vigorously that she appeared to be shaking it off — and said, —

"No, no. Father might find it out."

"Does your father know that he has given you that ring?"

"No, indeed. Father would compel me to wear it if he knew it."

"Well, then, Bella, why not return the ring? I will take it to him if you wish."

"Thank you," gratefully replied the young lady, and the smile with which this was said disclosed a very pretty row of teeth. "I think I will let you take the ring back. Perhaps he will take the hint, and not trouble me any more."

Now, whether owing to the tone in which these

words were spoken, or to the sudden disclosure of the pretty row of teeth, or to the smile which, in the silvery light of the night planet, certainly looked exceedingly engaging, and softened, in a wonderful manner, what of natural sharpness of expression there may have been in the lady's face, no one can say, yet, it was probably owing to one or all of these circumstances combined, that the young gentleman's manner most suddenly and thoroughly changed, and that in place of his late self-possession he appeared to be in the depths of embarrassment and mental distress; fidgeting uneasily upon the step, nervously feeling his fingers, and looking pleadingly at the man in the moon as if beseeching the kindly assistance of that pudding-faced individual.

Far be it from me to say that the young lady saw the sudden change in the young gentleman's demeanor. Perish the thought that she knew perfectly well what was the cause of the young man's distress, and that she rather enjoyed his confusion.

Let it simply be recorded that her eyes shone with a brighter light, and that her tongue moved with greater rapidity than ever, and that the pretty row of teeth and the engaging smile were called into requisition with unusual frequency.

Plucking up courage at last to interrupt her

animated flow of words, the young man stammered, "Bella, you cannot have been blind to — ah ——"

"Oh, do look at that cloud! Isn't it beautiful?"

What possible motive could have caused the lady to thus abruptly change the conversation can only be explained by the millions of her sisters who have acted similarly under similar circumstances.

"Bella, I cannot repress it. May — I ask whether — you could be happy — if — if — I mean to say — don't — don't you think it's a beautiful evening?"

Miserable subterfuge! Unpardonable coward! No wonder that the lady's eyes snapped and that the timid young gentleman hung his head. No wonder that the moon, ashamed to look upon his face, retreated behind a snowy bank of cloud, and that the old tin sign, disgusted with the whole proceedings, went off into a perfect spasm of angry squeaks and wails.

The necessity for further conversation was at this moment removed by the occurrence of a succession of complicated noises which proceeded from the hall of the house before which the couple were seated, and which gradually increased in volume and power.

Excitedly springing to his feet, the young gentleman began to ascend the steps, whether to invade the professor's domicile under the vague impression that something was happening in the house in which it was absolutely necessary that he should interfere, or whether simply to place himself before the closed door in the defiant attitude which tradition and the stage ascribe to the renowned Mr. Ajax, is still a matter of conjecture, since the young gentleman was immediately stopped in his valorous advance by the hand of the young lady, which was laid on his arm, and by the voice of the young lady, which exclaimed, "Oh, don't! It is nothing. It is only father and Brankey."

But any further entreaty to restrain the young gentleman from advancing was entirely unnecessary. For, precisely at this moment, the door suddenly opened and a stranger, propelled by an invisible force, dashed precipitately toward the young gentleman, whereupon they rolled down the steps and over each other upon the pavement in the most intimate manner imaginable.

Recovering from this unforeseen dismissal from his lady-love, the young gentleman hastily scrambled to his feet, and, securing his hat, which was gayly trundling along the street before a stiff breeze, turned and faced the scene of his disaster.

To his surprise his lady-love was nowhere to be

seen, while beneath the old tin sign, upon the topmost step stood a tall, broad-shouldered and heavily black-whiskered gentleman, who held in one hand a black bottle, and in the other a collar, which latter article enveloped the very red neck of a bland, smooth-faced gentleman of quite respectable proportions who was at this moment hopelessly intoxicated — as a continual silly smile upon his face, and an obstinate tendency upon the part of his legs to vacillate and fly off in all directions without the slightest excuse or warning, gave ample testimony.

The astonishment into which this sight had plunged the young gentleman was still further increased by the approach or rather the presence (since they were already present when he saw them, and must have made their appearance during his recent adventure) of three strangers; who, however, drawing nearer, proved to be our friends, Uncle Dan, Mr. Doolittle and Mr. Cribbler.

"There he is!" said Dick, raising his arm and pointing to the young gentleman, "there he is!"

Bob, for it was no other, was immediately surrounded by his friends.

"Dear me!" panted Uncle Dan, wiping the perspiration from his face with a blue handkerchief, "Is that you, Bob? How glad I am to see you!"

"Don't count your chickens before they are hatched," said Dick.

"Is it over, Bob?" eagerly inquired Harry. "Have you done it? Were you successful? Is it all over?"

"Now, hold on," said Bob, his comical self-assurance promptly asserting itself in the presence of his male friends. "What are you all driving at? One at a time now. What is the matter with you, and what are you after?"

"Say, Bob," said Dick, with genuine concern in the tone of his voice, "you haven't gone and thrown yourself away, have you?"

"Do I look like it, heh?" replied Bob. "Throw myself away! very likely. Next."

"Have you succeeded, Bob? Do tell us what ails you?" eagerly said Harry.

"Nothing ails me. Ails me, indeed! I'd like to know what ails *you* — you're so preciously mysterious about something. Uncle Dan, what's the matter? Dick, hush up! Harry, be still!"

"Well, the truth is, my boy," responded Uncle Dan, affectionately laying a hand on each of Bob's shoulders, "the fact is that your letter to Harry so alarmed us that we couldn't rest until we had hunted you up; and we are really anxious to know whether everything is all right."

Now, I am sure that the man in the moon had his revenge for having been so unmercifully bullied a short time before by Mr. Robert Sturdy; for that young man, strange to say, lost all self-possession, blushed, looked down at the pavement and behaved altogether in a painfully bashful and embarrassed manner.

"Well — no," he said, at length, speaking very slowly and reluctantly, —"things have not gone exactly right — I can't say that I have succeeded — it's no use — I haven't the courage — I might as well go to Texas and drive cattle — or fight Indians — the sooner it's over the better."

"Dear me! Dear me! Bob, my good fellow, if I can assist you in any way, — you know, Bob, you have my undivided sympathy — now, what is it?"

But Bob would not explain.

Dick, however, who had looked particularly bright and happy since Bob had confessed the failure of his enterprise, put his mouth close to Uncle Dan's ear and whispered a few words.

"Is that so?" exclaimed the good-natured gentleman, while his face brightened and his eyes twinkled, "why, I never thought of that. Bob, my dear boy, don't give up. Try again, 'faint heart never won,' you know. And I'll put in a good word for you with the professor. Dear me! Never despair, my boy, never despair."

Little Mr. Sturdy favored his good friend with a grateful glance, and, in the mingling of his emotions of renewed hope and gratitude to Uncle Dan, forgot to inquire how his friends had been able to find him or how they had known where to look for him.

Dick, however, winked confidentially at the man in the moon, while Harry smiled and mentally made a number of notes for future use in the Great American Novel, an enterprise of which no man knew the beginning and of which no man could predict the end.

Further conversation between the friends was interrupted by a grunt and a groan.

"Dear me!" exclaimed Uncle Dan, "what's that?"

This exclamation was instantly followed by a louder grunt and a deeper groan; whereupon the friends looked eagerly in the direction from whence the sounds proceeded, and beheld the tall, broad-shouldered gentleman with the black whiskers engaged in the interesting occupation of shaking the stout, smooth-faced gentleman with all his might.

"Dear me!" said Uncle Dan, again. "Who's that?"

"That," said Mr. Sturdy, "is Professor Bulbous —and Brankey."

"Is it possible," cried Uncle Dan. "Brankey. Dear me! Just the man I wanted to see!" and so saying he hurried forward while his companions followed.

CHAPTER VII.

In which Mr. Robert Sturdy is lamentably unsuccessful and Mr. Brankey comes to grief.

ELL, well, professor!" shouted Uncle Dan, as soon as he came within speaking distance, "what is the matter now? What has he done?"

Professor Bulbous only secured a firmer hold upon the object of his wrath, gave him a tremendous shake, which brought forth a correspondingly dismal groan, and in a ponderous, deep, gruff voice uttered the single monosyllable, "Beast!"

"Dear me!" exclaimed Uncle Dan, recoiling a step, "what a very forcible exclamation that is! I hope you don't mean it, Bulbous, I really do hope you don't mean it."

The professor, without paying the slightest attention to Uncle Dan or to his friends, who had ranged themselves in a semi-circle before him, repeated his violent exercise with the limp gentleman precisely as before, and forcibly ejaculated, "Sot!"

"I am very sorry for him, Bulbous, very sorry indeed," said Uncle Dan, compassionately.

"Sorry!" growled the professor, as if he had just this moment became aware of Uncle Dan's presence. "Sorry! He's the man to be sorry. Is he sorry? Not a bit of it. And never will be. Drunkard!"

Another shake followed, succeeded by another groan.

"Where is there a man," continued the professor, in a tone of the gruffest contempt, "who leaves his family to suffer for bread and victuals, while he lounges in a bar-room all day! Here he is. Look at him. Swillpot!"

The shake which followed fairly lifted the smooth-faced gentleman from the stairs.

"Dear me!" said Uncle Dan, "you will choke him to death."

"Serve him right," quoth Dick, softly. "Go in, professor!"

"Dick," said Uncle Dan, severely, "I am ashamed of you. When I see a man in such a position I pity him — with all my heart — I pity him. And you ought to pity him, Dick, and not condemn him."

All of Dick's face, with the exception of his left eye, received this rebuke with commendable gravity; but the left eye did wink and contract and expand a great many times in a most remarkable manner, while Dick's left elbow, suddenly propelled outward, came painfully in contact with Harry's side, causing that young gentleman to stagger against his friend Bob, who in turn staggered to the curbstone, where he brought up lovingly against a tree-box, with his nose between two of the bars.

Having expended his surplus energy with another good shaking up of the limp gentleman, the professor grunted and growled, "Where is there a man who drowns all his earnings in whiskey, disgraces himself and troubles everybody about him by being in a continual state of intoxication? Here he is. Look at him. Beer-glass!"

It seemed to afford the burly professor intense satisfaction to end every indignant outburst and begin every muscular shaking by uttering a forcible epithet expressive of his supreme disgust.

"Where is there a man who would let his wife and children starve, ay, and steal the clothes from their backs to take to the pawn-shop rather than deprive himself of his drams. Here is the man. Look at the monster. Slop-cart!"

"Bulbous," said Uncle Dan, venturing to touch the professor's hand — the one that held the black bottle — "you will hurt him, Bulbous. He can't understand you, my friend. Let him sit down on the steps. Come now — be easy with him."

"A man," continued the professor, just as if no interruption had occurred, "a man who gets kicked out of the bar-room after he is so drunk that he can't stand — a man who makes a beast and a sot of himself every day of his life — such a man ventures to crawl into my house, through the back door, and tries to tumble up-stairs in the dark, because he hasn't sense enough left to know that his own home is half a mile away. Look at him. Here he is. Whiskey-tub!"

"Dear me!" said Uncle Dan, "did he do that? Poor fellow!"

Some symptoms of life at this moment appearing in the inebriate gentleman's person, inasmuch as his unreliable legs, which had been ridiculously swaying and bending in all directions like the accommodating legs of a cheerful jumping-jack, began to make some feeble efforts to steady themselves, and his heavy eyelids began slowly and spasmodically to open, the little circle of spectators drew nearer, while the muscular professor held him out at arm's length and looked at him with a heavy frown, like a grim executioner waiting to hear the last word of his unfortunate victim.

The heavy lips slowly opened, and a voice grown

husky from the effect of innumerable potations, managed with great difficulty to articulate, " Bul — Bul — Bulb's ! "

" Well," grunted the professor, " Out with it. Punch-bowl ! "

" Bul — Bulb's," said the husky voice, with its painfully thick utterance, " what'll you — you take ? "

" Hear that, will you ? Hear that ? " cried the professor, waving the black bottle around his head, " hear that ! The first thing he thinks of and the last thing he thinks of — in his cups and out of his cups — is drink, drink, drink. Rum-flask ! "

" You must make some allowance for him, Bulbous," said tender-hearted Uncle Dan — " he doesn't know what he is saying."

" Who comes here?
A grenadier.
What does he want?
A pot of beer,"

sang a voice in a low muffled tone.

Uncle Dan turned his mild, reproving gaze upon his three friends, but they presented faces of the most innocent composure, and it was impossible to decide who had relieved himself of this charming and poetical effusion. So that Uncle Dan could only administer his intended rebuke in a general way, saying, "My young friends, we should never make sport of the misfortunes of our fellow-men."

"Misfortune!" growled the deep-voiced professor, giving the victim such a poke between the shoulders with the black bottle that it made him wink and set the unreliable legs in motion again, jumping-jack fashion. "Misfortune! Bosh! I call it appetite. I call it selfishness. I call it stupid and unrelieved blockheadism — out and out. That's what it is. Beer-keg!"

Certain premonitory signs again appearing to herald another effort upon Mr. Brankey's part to be heard — the doctor desisted in his energetic operation of shaking him up, and held him up at arm's length as before.

"Bul — Bul — Bulb's," said the husky voice, with great difficulty, "I'm — I'm — friend o' yours."

"Oh, you are — are you?" grunted Professor Bulbous. "Well, my friend, I'll take a friend's privilege with you and give you a piece of my mind. I'll shake some sense into you before I'm through. Grog-cup!"

"Never say — say die. Here's luck. Bul— Bul — Bulb's — your bit — bitters 'r' th' best I ever — er tasted."

Dick winked, Harry smiled, Bob chuckled softly,

even Uncle Dan could not help rubbing his hands in quiet appreciation of Mr. Brankey's remark.

But Professor Bulbous could only wave the black bottle over the victim's head in speechless indignation.

"First dram — ever took — hic! was your bit — bitters, Bulb's — ten years ago — tasted good — three times day — 'cordin' prescription — Friends, Bulb's — you an' I — what'll you take, Bulb's — whiskey straight? — Hooray — Hoo ——"

"What!" shouted the angry professor, at length, "what!"

"N' you never g' back on friend," continued Mr. Brankey, helplessly rolling his head from side to side, "neither will I. You're bit — bitters 'snothin' but — hic! — wintergreen an' rye whiskey — Bulb's — friends — you 'n I — Hoo ——"

Mr. Brankey's further utterance was cut short by a tremendous shake.

"Villian! Liar! Brandy-soak!" thundered the professor.

"No 'fence — hic — Bulb's — no — no 'fence, my friend."

"Offence!" cried the enraged professor. "Offence! *I* teach you how to drink! *I* make a sot of you! Say *I* fed you ten years ago on a vile mixture of wintergreen and whiskey! And then say no offence! Brew-vat! *Whiskey-jug!* ALE-BOTTLE!"

And having thus given vent to his overpowering indignation, the professor threw poor Brankey from him like a wet rag, bounced into the house and shut the door with a resounding slam. No sooner was the support of the professor's strong right hand removed from Mr. Brankey's collar than that gentleman's knees demonstrated their utter uselessness for any practical purpose, except getting their owner into trouble, by promptly doubling under him, whereby Mr. Brankey's body was compelled to tumble forward and Mr. Brankey's head plunged unceremoniously against the third button of Uncle Dan's vest and nearly knocked the breath out of that estimable gentleman.

In truth Uncle Dan would certainly have fallen to the ground had not Dick fortunately caught his arm and assisted him in recovering his balance.

"Dear me!" exclaimed Uncle Dan, "that was very kind of you, Dick, very kind, indeed. But what a very rude gentleman the professor is, to be sure! I never saw anything like it. Dear me! Look at Mr. Brankey! Get up, my dear sir, get up, I beg of you!"

Mr. Brankey was prostrate before Uncle Dan, gracefully balanced upon his knees and his nose, and had the appearance of an eastern devotee making his morning obeisance to the sun.

Seeing that he paid no attention to Uncle Dan's request to rise, Dick took a firm hold of his collar, after the manner of Professor Bulbous, and pulled him up.

"Dear me! What shall we do with him now?" anxiously inquired Uncle Dan.

"The only thing we can do, or rather the only alternatives we have," said Bob, speaking with his usual decision, "are either to let him remain here until he sobers off or to give him in charge of a policeman."

"We will do neither," replied Uncle Dan, hastily, "and I am sure your good heart did not prompt either of these suggestions." ·

"The cellar-door's open. Put him down in the professor's cellar," said Harry.

"Among the coal-dirt and rats and mice — impossible!" answered Uncle Dan.

"Take him to the river and cool him off," said Dick.

"Yes, duck him," said Bob, laughing.

"Good!" exclaimed Harry. "What a splendid item that will be for my novel! I must remember it."

"Young gentlemen," rejoined Uncle Dan, "you

must be jesting. Such remarks could not have been seriously meant. No, no. The only thing that we can do with this unfortunate gentleman is to take him home. Dick, you know where he lives, lead the way. Harry, you support him on the left, I will hold him on the right, and Bob, you must follow and help us get him into the house. So, so, Mr. Brankey. Try to steady yourself, sir; one foot at a time, sir; we can't possibly get you home if you persist in raising both feet from the ground at the same time; that's better. So — now then — off we go. Dear me! Dear me!"

And in this novel manner the little procession took its way along the quiet streets towards Mr. Brankey's humble home, only disturbed now and then by the ominous sound of a policeman's club striking on the pavement, or the angry barking of some watchful dog.

. .

Later, on the same night, there crept cautiously within the shelter of the tree-boxes, a little short, dark shadow, which paused before the creaking tin sign, and from which proceeded two or three peculiar signals whistled in a very careful and subdued manner; and a moment later one of the professor's window-blinds opened very slowly about half-an-inch and disclosed a long, slender finger which beckoned in a very guarded and mysterious way.

The shadow, creeping softly from the shelter of the tree-boxes, glided swiftly across the moonlit space to the open shutter, and revealed the bushy hair and well-known lineaments of our friend Mr. Robert Sturdy. While at the same time a sharp voice, speaking in a low whisper and saying, "Well — you've come back, have you?" was proof that the owner of the slender beckoning finger was Miss Bella Bulbous.

"Yes," said Bob, standing on tiptoe, "I came to get the ring."

"Oh, yes. I forgot to give it to you."

"It was not your fault. You did not have time. Did your father see me?"

"No. Well that he didn't. He was angry enough to eat me when he came in. Bad boy!"

The last expression was addressed to Bob in consequence of his having raised his face by a powerful effort, with the aid of his hands resting upon the window sill, to a level with the slender finger, which he had timidly kissed.

"Here's the ring," said the lady, dropping it out of the window into Bob's palm, "and now you must leave me, because father is still up. And if he hears us he'll be *so* angry!"

"I'll go in a minute," said Bob, raising his eyes pleadingly, "but I must say something, Bella, that has been on my mind for a long time; something that has robbed me of sleep night after night;— something that ——"

"Papa's coming!"

"A moment more! Bella, from the first day I saw you ——"

"He's at the door!"

"All I want to say is, Bella, that—that I constantly think of ——"

"Good night! Run away! He'll see you surely!"

"In short, Bella—I must tell you that I love ——"

A door opened suddenly—a deep grunt was heard and in a second the slender finger was withdrawn, the shutters were closed, and poor Bob stood upon the silent street, dejected and alone.

"Failed again," he muttered bitterly as he wandered slowly away — "failed again. Just when I picked up the courage to do it, too. I'll never be able to say it again. She'd laugh at me. I know what I'm going to do now. I'm going to Texas to drive cattle."

And with this gloomy resolve the disconsolate

lover went home and passed another sleepless night.

And just as Bob tumbled moodily into bed he heard the bell from a neighboring steeple strike the hour — One !

CHAPTER VIII.

Mr. Poldertot is surprised in more ways than one. — And Mr. Sluff develops talent as an orator under unusual circumstances.

IT was a very warm, uncomfortable, sullen Sunday afternoon. The sun shone down so hotly upon the dusty town that every living thing upon which it shed its burning rays wilted and lost strength, except the countless flies which were out in swarms and acted as if they were in a desperate league with the scorching sun to drive everybody mad. Dogs in open doorways, covered alley-ways, or under awnings, lay with mouths wide open and tongues protruding, panting with all their might. Street-car horses upon their monotonous rounds tugged painfully at the overcrowded cars, while the low drooping of their heads and the big flakes of foam that fell from their tortured mouths and sweating sides gave evidence of how terribly they suffered. Leaves of plants and flowers hung half withered on their stems and stalks, and none of them moved, for not the slightest breeze was stirring. Pedestrians fumed and perspired and fretted as they passed along, eagerly availing themselves of such little shade as the broiling streets afforded, seeking anxiously for some cool, refreshing spot, and finding none.

One stout gentleman in particular felt the oppressive heat to such a degree that he sought at intervals of two or three minutes the shelter of an awning or a thick-leaved tree, and there stood a few moments fanning himself vigorously with a palm-leaf fan, and mopping his reddened face with a handkerchief already wet with perspiration.

At such times the stout, red-faced gentleman would look back earnestly, and then wistfully forward as if mentally calculating the difference between the distance that he had already come, and the distance he had still to go.

That these reflections were of a satisfactory nature may be supposed from the fact that the gentleman's inflamed countenance assumed a somewhat brighter expression after each of these silent calculations, and that he began to look forward with more frequency, fixing his eyes upon one certain spot in the distance, as one may do who sees his goal before him and knows that he will reach it very soon.

And such, in truth, was the case; for, having

traversed some twelve or fifteen blocks from the point where we will suppose that he was first introduced to the reader in this chapter, the stout gentleman drew near a very dingy, very dusty, and very much neglected-looking building of a rectangular form, made of brick, and surmounted by a tapering pile of the same material over the front wall, probably intended to represent a steeple, while a smaller pile of a similar shape surmounted the rear wall, the object and use of which no man had ever known.

Approaching the open door of this building, through which could be heard the hum of many voices, mingled with the melancholy notes of a wheezy organ, evidently played by an unskilful performer, the gentleman placed his foot upon the stone doorstep, preparatory to entering, when he was arrested by a sight which caused him considerable surprise.

"Dear me!" exclaimed the stout gentleman, thereby revealing himself to the gentle reader as our veritable friend and hero, Uncle Dan. "What a very large attendance we have to-day! And most all of them men! Why, I'm sure we have had only a quarter of this number present for the last three months. Dear me! Where can they have come from?"

The sound of the well-known voice of Uncle Dan, who had unconsciously uttered these words aloud, had an instantaneous effect upon the assembly in the room. The hum of voices, although not altogether hushed, was considerably modified, and the unskilful performer precipitately retiring from the wheezy organ, the sound of that doleful instrument was heard no more.

Seeing that he had been observed, Uncle Dan hesitated no longer, but boldly entered the hall and presented his inflamed but ever good-humored face in one of the aisles, and, pleasantly smiling, advanced until he reached an elevated platform where his chair awaited him.

For, be it known, this assemblage was a meeting of the friends and members of the Band of Hope, of which Uncle Dan was the beloved and honored president; and the room in which this meeting was held was the lecture-room, Sunday-school room, regular school-room, prayer-meeting room, singing-school room, and general utility room of a German congregation, who worshipped in the church-hall above, and, in consequence of the various purposes for which it was used was in a state of hopeless dilapidation.

Owing to the glowing representations of our noble Uncle Dan, respecting the immense benefits to be derived from, and the unlimited good which could be accomplished with such an institution as the Band of Hope, or, in other words, a temperance Sunday School, the room had been placed at his disposal, with all its plaster-broken walls, its smoke-covered ceiling, its rude platform, its hard, uncomfortable benches, hacked by the knives, and splashed with the ink-blots of unnumbered tow-headed urchins, and its lugubrious organ, which never was heard but it sounded as if it was playing its own funeral dirge.

As Uncle Dan permitted his gaze to rest upon the increased attendance, and therefore saw scores of new faces — many of them evidently in the greatest need of the peculiar ministrations of a Band of Hope — Uncle Dan's heart was filled with a mingled feeling of pride, satisfaction, and thankfulness. It is true that the Band presented its usual array of bright-faced children, many of them prepared with a long selection of either poetry or prose, highly eulogistic of temperance, which they were prepared to deliver with the peculiarly charming and unstudied grace of childhood, as soon as the exercises should begin. It is also true that the Band was well provided with leaders, whose energies upon this hot, sweltering afternoon were largely employed in the exhausting labor of fanning themselves and trying to keep the restless little feet in their classes from kicking too often and impatiently against the benches in front. Neither can it be denied that Mr. Sluff, the superintendent, a medium-sized gentleman, with a face like a full moon, and a suit of clothes upon which the tailor had apparently expended all his ingenuity in order to make as complete and gross a misfit as could be devised by the mind of man, was present, as was also Mr. Smillage, the vice-president, a man with a red face, a tremendous red moustache, which completely covered his mouth, and of which he was intensely and uninterruptedly proud, a pair of piercing eyes — a man, in short, wearing altogether the fierce look of a corsair, but really possessing the gentle disposition of a lamb ; Mr. Little, the assistant superintendent (a man with a solid frown, who scolded the children whenever he could, to the great disgust of Uncle Dan), who came out strong in leading the singing by beating the palm of his left hand with a song-book held in his right, and yelling his way through every tune with such a frightful expression upon his face that the uninitiated believed him to be in convulsions, until having fascinated everybody else into silence, the wheezy organ and himself completed the song with a most doleful wail and a blood-curdling cry; Mr. Fritters, the organist, a young gentleman still in his teens (but already a great favorite with the young ladies, also in their teens), whose musical education was evidently in its earliest stage of development, as the indescribable and inharmonious complications extracted from the long-suffering organ repeatedly testified; Mr. Bromley, the first usher, a stout young man, in a continual state of ill-humor, which he manifested in growls and grumblings upon the most trifling occasions, although everybody knew that he never meant a word of what he said; and Mr. Seldon, the second usher, a short, lean young man, the bosom friend of Mr. Bromley, constantly endeavoring to arouse Mr. Bromley's ire, and, having succeeded, pretending to soothe him in a quiet and peculiar manner, which only resulted in adding fuel to the flames.

All these were present engaged in their several duties as well as the extraordinary warmth of the day would permit, all these were present I say; but the strangers outnumbered them two to one — even though one had counted with the officers, Mr. Robert Sturdy, the treasurer, Mr. Harry Cribbler, the secretary, and the general confidant, friend and assistant of the members of the band — that genteel gentleman of leisure, Mr. Richard Doolittle, who had not yet put in an appearance.

There being still a few moments to spare before the hour for beginning the exercises, it occurred to Uncle Dan that he could employ those few moments very profitably in personally welcoming some of the strangers and making them feel at home. It was a noble thought; and no sooner had it presented itself to the mind of its great progenitor than Uncle Dan arose and descending from his platform with a smile of benevolence, and, with a light of hearty welcome and good-will shining through his glittering spectacles, advanced along the aisle on the right to the centre of the room where the strangers were congregated. Naturally Uncle Dan accosted the first stranger toward whom his steps led him, and who happened to be a very fleshy young gentleman, with a particularly rubicund nose and attired in garments which the laundry had certainly not had possession of for a long time.

He was, moreover, so wet with perspiration that his linen coat was nothing but a large moist sheet of an uncertain color; and at the same time there hovered about him such an atmosphere of the strongest "old rye" and the worst tobacco that his immediate neighbors had generously moved away, so that he sat quite alone in solitary glory.

"My dear sir," said Uncle Dan, approaching with extended hand, "how do you do? I am glad to see you here. I bid you welcome, sir; welcome to our Band."

The strange gentleman was so affected by this kind welcome that he could say nothing and only shook Uncle Dan's hand earnestly and winked in a strange and mysterious manner.

"I hope you will like our exercises and that you will come often," said Uncle Dan.

The gentleman continued to wring Uncle Dan's hand affectionately and wink mysteriously for several moments. At length as Uncle Dan tried to release his hand in order to present it to another stranger, the gentleman, speaking with a thick utterance, said, —

"I say, Mis'r Pal'rtot!"

"Sir?" said Uncle Dan.

"I say — lemme see you — will you? just a minute — private," and then he winked again, mysteriously as before.

"I will be glad to see you after the Band is dismissed, and if I can do anything for you," said Uncle Dan, "I will do it with the greatest pleasure."

The gentleman appeared satisfied, released Uncle Dan's hand, and ensconcing himself in the corner of the bench promptly went to sleep, while Uncle Dan, almost overpowered by the combined fumes of bad tobacco and worse whiskey passed on to the next stranger. This was a man with a sallow complexion, straight black hair and a shabby genteel suit of clothes. This man received Uncle Dan's welcome with tearful gratitude and a most courteous manner.

After a short conversation he too requested the favor of a moment's private conversation with Uncle Dan. Uncle Dan bade him remain after the children were dismissed, and passed on to the third and the fourth and the fifth and so on to the twentieth stranger, all of whom, to his amazement requested the favor of a short conversation with Uncle Dan in private.

In a state of wondering surprise, Uncle Dan returned to the platform, and, ringing a small silver-plated bell, called the Band to order, and announced the hour for opening the exercises. These exercises generally consisted of a short prayer either by Uncle Dan, or Mr. Sluff, the superintendent, — the reading of a portion of the Scriptures by Mr. Snillage, reading of the minutes of the previous meeting by the secretary, the questions and responses from the ritual — (the latter consisting mainly of selected passages of Scripture in reference to the use of wine and strong drink) in which all the officers, leaders, and members took part, recitations by the children, interspersed with numerous temperance songs, and occasionally a short address by a friend of the Band, invited guest or distinguished visitor. It must not be forgotten, however, that the principal feature of the exercises was the taking of the pledge by the new converts in these words, repeated after the superientendent : —

"I solemnly pledge myself to abstain from the use of all spirituous or malt liquors, wine or cider, as a beverage ; from the use of tobacco in all its forms and from all profanity."

Having thus briefly described the exercises that generally took place, it is not necessary to enter upon a detailed description of the exercises of this particular day, for they were very similar to those described above, — with one exception, however — a great exception, and the record of which cannot here be omitted, since it affords one of the greatest proofs of the love and esteem in which their worthy president was held by every member of the Band of Hope.

It has been noticed that Robert, Dick and Harry were late, inasmuch as they had not arrived when the exercises began ; but fifteen minutes later, just as the words of a temperance song, —

> "Water — water; pure, sparkling, free,
> Oh, 'tis water bright,
> In its silver light,
> And the crystal fount for me,"

were being sung, the three friends came noiselessly into the room, Harry with a package in his arms.

A smile came over the faces of the officers and leaders and some of the older scholars as they saw it, and as Harry deposited it carefully in a remote corner behind the organ, almost every eye was turned that way with a glance of eager expectation.

The pleasant hour at length was over — like so many other pleasant hours — a thing of the past; Uncle Dan reading from the ritual had solemnly pronounced the words, —

"And now the time has come for us to part and to go forth cheerfully unto our duties. What lesson should we carry with us that we may be good and wise?"

And then the whole Band of Hope reciting in unison had responded, —

"We should do unto others as we would have that others should do unto us." The Lord's Prayer had been repeated in concert, and Uncle Dan was just preparing to dismiss the band, when Mr.

Sluff, the superintendent, spoke and begged the members of the Band and the visitors present to be seated for a few moments.

There was a great rustling of dresses, shuffling of feet, nudging of elbows, exchanging of significant glances, hurried whisperings and strange smiles before the people had again taken their seats.

When quiet was somewhat restored, Mr. Sluff, the superintendent, turning his back to the people and his face toward Uncle Dan, opened his mouth, and to Mr. Poldertot's great astonishment addressed him in the following words:—

" Mr. President, -- Most Respected, Esteemed, and Honored Sir,—

" To one who has had the great good fortune of being intimately associated with you, sir, in the direction and supervision of this, our beloved Band of Hope, and, knowing as well as I do, the sincerity, the self-denial and the love which has accompanied your disinterested labors in its behalf, the task which has been allotted to me at this moment becomes one which my heart and mind willingly and voluntarily transform into a heartfelt pleasure — a pure and unalloyed labor of love. (A murmur of approval from the Band.) Most humbly do I acknowledge that more eloquent lips than mine could have been chosen to speak in my place to-day and to say what is my duty and my pleasure to say. But that any one could have devoted to this pleasant duty a heart more sincere, more happy and more ready in conveying to you, our cherished president, the unanimous well wishes and the undivided love of all the members here, I deny, sir, I most emphatically deny.

"Sir, it becomes then my duty to say that the members of the Band of Hope have chosen this time and this method of publicly informing you of the great joy with which they have witnessed your untiring zeal and ceaseless energy in its behalf, and to thank you from the bottom of every heart that beats within the sound of my voice for all that you have done for us. We thank you, sir, for your disinterested devotion to the noble cause of temperance ; we thank you, sir, for the sincerity of every act of your official life ; for the encouragement which you have given us by timely counsel and assistance ; for the self-denial constantly manifested in sacrificing your personal ease and comfort in order that you might bestow your valuable time and presence upon us, a struggling, feeble company, and, sir, we thank you, with a deeper gratitude than we can express for those who by your own efforts have been induced to abandon those vile habits which in the course of time would assuredly have led them to ruin — ruin of health, ruin of wealth and ruin of soul. (*Profound sensation.*)

"But, sir, my words are weak. Especially are they weak when compared with the strong feelings which they are intended to portray.

"The Band of Hope, sir, knew the inadequacy of words upon this occasion, and so (turning quickly and receiving from Harry the mysterious bundle, which, devoid of its wrappings, proved to be a magnificent family Bible, bound in morocco and edged with gilt) it desires as a slight token of its love and esteem to present to you this book, whose blessed precepts and divine commands you have so faithfully endeavored to inculcate.

"And, sir, with this humble proof of its unbounded affection, the Band of Hope wishes you a long, a prosperous and a happy life."

A loud murmur of satisfaction and approval greeted the close of Mr. Sluff's happy address, the greatest sensation occurring amongst the ladies who could not refrain from exclaiming, — "Beautiful!" "That's good!" "Charming!" "Couldn't have been better!" "Eloquent language!" "Very appropriate, I am sure!" "Heavenly!" "Mr. Poldertot deserves every word of it." "And more, too," while they cast upon the president glances of the most melting tenderness.

To say that Uncle Dan was overwhelmed by this unexpected evidence of the affection of his fellow-members would be but feebly expressing his state of mind.

For a few moments he could only stare helplessly over the crowded room. At length, arising slowly, poor Uncle Dan, turning his spectacles around back and forth between his nervous fingers, and stammering, said, —

"I — I — really, my kind friends — this — this — is so unexpected — that I can only — only thank you. I am afraid that — you have — ah — you have overrated my humble services. Certainly the — the pleasure I have received — the — the precious friendship which I have here, and do here enjoy, more than repay — much — much more than repay me for the little that I have done in this — in this glorious cause. But, Mr. Sluff — and friends — when in the course of human events — it — it becomes — dear me! what am I saying? I am all upset — you must excuse me — well — well! I can only say, ladies and gentlemen and children — dear friends, all — I thank you. And I mean that from the bottom of my heart."

And as Uncle Dan sat down utterly overcome such a nodding and whispering and rustling immediately took place that it is certain, had it been any other day but Sunday, Uncle Dan would have been greeted with round after round of the most vociferous applause.

Seeing that there was nothing else to be done, Mr. Sluff arose and said, —

"The Band is dismissed."

And the Band in obedience to his announcement promptly resolved itself into its component parts as individuals, and laughingly overflowing into the aisles, rippled and hummed and rustled and gushed through the doorway into the open air. But the solid phalanx of strangers stolidly remained in their places determined to have a few minutes of private conversation with Uncle Dan; the strangest feature of this strange affair being that each one of these unknown persons evidently regarded all the others with anxiety and suspicion. And as this chapter is already long enough, we must reserve the explanation of the mystery for the next.

CHAPTER IX.

Mr. Doolittle again assists Uncle Dan; and, sociably inclined, interviews Mr. Rolf Seppeld.

IN the meantime Uncle Dan was lost in profound reverie. When at last he aroused himself from the happy train of reflections which had been produced by the pleasant occurrences narrated in the last chapter, he gave evidence of returning consciousness to present surroundings by a long, deep sigh and his favorite exclamation, "Dear me!" uttered slowly and distinctly four times in succession.

Raising his eyes, which had for several minutes been staring at vacancy, he became aware that the room was being rapidly deserted by the members of the Band, and that, in short, there only remained the numerous strangers, the officers, a few of the leaders and his tried and trusted bodyguard — Mr. Sturdy, Mr. Cribbler and Mr. Doolittle.

Bob and Harry were engaged in a conversation with two young ladies, Mr. Doolittle stood in the centre of the room lazily leaning against the end of one of the benches, having his arms folded and complacently listening to the remarks of a darkfeatured gentleman who held a ring in his hand, which he regarded with a forbidding frown; and from the manner in which he glanced vindictively at the group in which Bob and Harry figured and shook his head or his fist it may be supposed that the excited remarks which he addressed to the imperturbable Dick were not at all complimentary to either one or both of these gentlemen. Mr. Sluff, Mr. Smillage, Mr. Little and Mr. Fritters were gathered around the amiable Mr. Bromley, who, with his coat-sleeves pushed up, his hat on the back of his head, and a portentous frown upon his countenance, was declaring in a loud voice and with many violent gesticulations (to the imminent danger of the heads and noses of his superior officers) that he was not going to stand it, that he had been imposed on long enough, and that if Ben Seldon thought he could make a cat's paw of Mr. William Bromley, Mr. William Bromley would let him know that he was very much mistaken — winding up these startling declarations with the severe announcement that he would be everlastingly golderswashed if he didn't clap a stopper on his friend at the next provocation in very short order; while Mr. Ben Seldon lightly hovered upon the outskirts of the distinguished circle, and, with a peculiar twitching of his mouth, begged Mr. Bromley to keep cool, and to forgive him this time, and he would never do it again, and to deal with him gently and spare his young heart, and to be kind to the orphan, and offered many more such beautiful and touching recommendations, all of which seemed to have an effect on Mr. Bromley which was the very reverse of soothing. Meanwhile, the strangers waited patiently in their seats — still suspiciously regarding one another and now and then casting appealing glances toward Uncle Dan, thus mutely urging him to grant them the private audience which they had so earnestly solicited; seeing which Uncle Dan was immediately conscience-stricken.

"Dear me!" thought Mr. Poldertot, "what a forgetful being I am! Here are all these people waiting to speak to me, and here am I deliberately wasting their time by idling in my chair. Very careless of me — very careless, indeed."

And with these self-accusing thoughts in his mind, Uncle Dan hastily left the platform and advanced toward the ruddy-nosed gentleman to whom he had first promised an interview.

To the great disgust of this gentleman, however, Uncle Dan's progress was intercepted by the towering form of Dick, who stood directly in his way.

"Uncle Dan," said Dick, grasping the lapels of the president's coat and thus effectually preventing him from moving on, "I want to speak to you."

"Certainly, Dick, certainly — as soon as I am at liberty — shortly. At present I want to speak to that gentleman in the third seat back."

"You mean," said Dick, speaking in his naturally slow and indolent manner, "that the gentleman in the third seat back wants to speak to *you.*"

"Well, yes; that would perhaps be more correct, but ——"

"And I wouldn't be surprised," observed Dick, shutting one eye and gently feeling the lapels of the president's coat with his thumbs and forefingers, as if endeavoring to ascertain the texture and quality of the goods, "to learn that the gentleman in the fourth seat back is also waiting to say a few words to you in private."

"Precisely — precisely, Dick — the gentlemen are anxious to see me — and it is getting late."

"And if I was a betting man," continued Dick, without paying the slightest attention to Uncle

Dan's gentle efforts to free himself, "I should like to wager that the gentlemen in the other back seats have a similarly urgent desire to interview the Honorable Mr. Poldertot."

"Why, dear me! So they have, Dick, so they have."

"On a matter unknown?"

"On a matter unknown."

"Well, then," said Dick with the air of a man who has succeeded in making the solution of a mystery all the more startling by delaying the explanation as long as possible, "read that."

Uncle Dan carefully adjusted his spectacles and brought them to bear upon a small printed slip of paper which Dick had handed him.

"Dear me! Dear me!" said Uncle Dan, as soon as he had read it.

"Just so," said Dick.

"The advertisement!"

"The advertisement."

"And you think that these men ——"

"Are candidates for a clerkship."

"In my store?"

"In your store."

"But — dear me — Dick, I never attend to business on Sunday."

"That's what I thought."

"And I can't possibly talk to these people to-day about this."

"Just so."

"But what can I do?"

"Don't talk to them."

"I promised to, Dick." And any one who knew how sacred Uncle Dan regarded every promise, and at the same time how loth he was to attend to any secular business upon the Sabbath, could appreciate the predicament in which that conscientious gentleman found himself.

"Ah," said Dick, suddenly arousing into activity — "just wait here a minute, Uncle Dan; I'll attend to it."

"Hold — Dick — Dick! What are you going to do?"

But Dick only put the forefinger of his right hand on his mouth in token of silence, and, turning without giving Uncle Dan time to remonstrate, approached the gentleman with the red nose.

What Dick said to this gentleman must forever remain a secret, since he never condescended to enlighten any one upon the subject. But it was observed with surprise that Dick approached the stranger and shook him cordially by the hand and then engaged in a whispered conversation with him, and that at the expiration of a few moments the stranger nodded his head as if convinced of the truth of some proposition which Dick had presented. And a few seconds thereafter the stranger was seen to rise slowly and slouch reluctantly out of the room.

The same mysterious method sufficed to induce another stranger to follow the first, and then another and another until five or six of them had left the room, whereupon the rest of the unknown company, probably coming to the conclusion that it was useless to wait any longer, arose in a body and disconsolately followed the advance guard.

Uncle Dan was exceedingly grateful to Dick for this signal service, and if he had not himself accepted an invitation to dine with Mr. Sluff, in company with Mr. Smillage, Mr. Little and Mr. Fritters, he would certainly have invited Dick to go home with him, forgetful of the fact that the presiding genius of his home, Aunt Prudence, was absent, and that he was altogether unprepared to entertain a guest.

Now, dismissing Uncle Dan, who is on his way in an eastwardly direction with his friends, allowing Bob and Harry to quietly wend their way to the north as they gallantly escort Miss Bella Bulbous and a graceful, dark-eyed young lady, who is a leader of the Band, a bosom friend of Bella's, and whose name is Ella Trigg, over the gutters and the sunken alleys, catching a parting glance in the south of Mr. Ben Seldon's coat-tails as they vanish around a distant corner with Mr. William Bromley in hot pursuit, we will accompany Dick for a few moments, and learn what he had to say to the dark-featured gentleman, as with arms linked they proceeded in a westwardly direction until they reach Carr Park, which they enter, and where they mingle with a promiscuous stream of humanity circling round and round a shabby little fountain like moths around a candle.

"Rolf," said Dick, coaxingly, as they circled slowly about, "what is the necessity for getting angry about it?"

"Well," rejoined his companion, frowning heavily, "you'd find reason enough to be angry, let me tell you, if you were in my place."

"I don't see it," retorted Dick. "If Miss Bulbous does not wish to keep your ring she has a perfect right to return it. That's one of woman's inalienable rights and ought to be so guaranteed to her by — by the constitution."

"But, look here!" said the dark-featured gentleman, fiercely, "if you loved a woman ——"

"Tut — tut!" said Dick, shaking his head with an expression of the greatest disgust.

"And you had paid her every attention, and she had received presents from you, and all that, don't you think you would be mad to have a ring returned without the slightest explanation?"

"Not at all," said Dick, calmly, "it wouldn't trouble me in the least."

"Well, it does me. And what's more, I don't propose to be jilted in this way."

"Bravo!" said Dick. "What will you do? Kidnap her, like a brigand — or drown her in a sack, like a Turk?"

"There are ways," said the gentleman, darkly, "in which a foolish woman can be made sensible, even in the nineteenth century, and she will find that I am not to be thwarted with impunity."

"But, man alive!" cried Dick, "what do you intend to do, Seppeld?"

"I intend," said Mr. Seppeld, "to marry Bella Bulbous."

"Poor Bella! sad indeed thy fate!" thought Dick. Then he said aloud, "But suppose she refuses to have anything to do with you — what then?"

"She will change her mind."

"Ah!" said Dick, "let's sit down."

They edged their way through the crowd which appeared to be constantly growing larger, and made their way to one of the iron settees. Here they reclined for a few moments in silence, watching the human tide as it came and went in its irregular ebb and flow.

Suddenly, as if an idea which demanded immediate attention had just entered his mind, Rolfh Seppeld straightened himself into an erect posture and said, sharply, "Doolittle!"

Dick, who had just taken an easy position, with his head thrown back, calmly surveyed the heavens, before making any reply to this abrupt address; and at length, when Mr. Seppeld was upon the point of again uttering his name, drawled in that slow, provoking manner which he could assume so easily, "Well?"

"Doolittle, I want to ask you a question."

"Ye – es?" said Dick, still deliberately examining the sky, "fire–a–wa–ay."

"Do you think," inquired Mr. Seppeld, while a darker expression than usual gathered over his face, "that Bob Sturdy means anything by his attentions to Bella Bulbous?"

Grasping the iron settee with one hand, Dick pulled himself slowly into an upright position, and then responded with the careful manner and tone of a judge who is rendering an important decision upon an exceedingly delicate subject, "let — me —

see. Does he — or does he not? The only thing I can do or suggest, Seppeld, is — to give you a piece of advice."

"Indeed. Well — what is it?"

"Ask Bob."

And having thus happily disposed of the question without committing himself to an opinion, Dick gently settled back again into his former position with his face to the sky.

"Well," said Mr. Seppeld, rising and pulling his hat down low over his forehead, "I have no questions to ask of Bob Sturdy. But when you see him you can warn him from me to let the young lady alone. It will be better for him and better for her."

"May I be permitted to ask," said Dick, lightly tapping the ends of his fingers together, "as a friend and a brother, you know, are you engaged to the young lady? No harm, my friend; I only ask for information."

Bending down so that his lips were near Dick's ear, Mr. Seppeld whispered, "Doolittle, I'll tell you something in confidence. We are not engaged yet, but I expect that we shall be soon. I have the professor under my thumb, and he won't dare to refuse his consent. He must make her marry me, mind, and if he don't, I'll crush him. Yes, sir,

I'll crush him. If Bella Bulbous" (sinking his voice to a still more impressive whisper) "knew what I know, she would marry me to-morrow."

"Then, why don't you tell her?"

"Because the time has not come — my plans are not quite completed."

"That is to say," observed Dick, "the apple is not quite ripe."

"Exactly — you understand me. I tell you this in confidence, Doolittle, so that you may see the necessity of keeping Bob Sturdy away from Bella Bulbous."

"Just so;" said Dick. "You won't forget to send me your cards, Seppeld?"

"Certainly not. What's that? Rain? So it is. Come, go home with me, Doolittle. No? Well, then I must go alone; and you'd better hurry home, too, or you'll get soaking wet. Good evening."

"Good evening," said Dick; and as he arose from his recumbent posture and passed out of the park he might have been heard to mutter, "The apple is too green, eh? I wonder whether any bad boy will pick the apple before it is ripe. Well — well — green apples are good, sometimes; and what a novel and exhilarating exercise it would be to shake the tree!"

And with this reflection in his mind, Dick left the

park, hastily boarded a Sixteenth-street car and rode homewards. And soon thereafter a brilliant flash of lightning illuminated the darkening streets, a crashing clap of thunder followed, and the mad rain, released from its confinement, came dashing down in slanting torrents.

CHAPTER X.

The exciting adventures connected with the loss of a turtle-dove.

THE light of Monday morning quickly making its way over that celebrated thoroughfare called Benton street, and peeping brightly through the partly open shutters of Uncle Dan's home, found that gentleman still snoring peacefully in bed.

There it found him, and there it beheld him three hours afterward in the same happily oblivious condition, still, as has been already mentioned once before, snoring peacefully in bed. The circumstance was one which merits special notice and attention. Not that the sight of a stout, middle-aged gentleman, with an exceedingly full, round, and ruddy face, snoring peacefully in bed (as has been stated), while his arms are thrown over his head upon the pillow and his nightcap is perched rakishly over one eye, is one to attract any particular attention. Since it may be truthfully observed that the race of stout gentlemen have a peculiarly happy faculty of sleeping, as has been pointedly remarked, like a top; though in what respect a top is supposed to have a greater power of indulging in somnolency than any other toy, say a doll-baby or a rocking-horse, for instance, is, and always has been, a mystery — unless it be a humming-top, in which case some connection may possibly be traced in the similarity of the noise it makes while spinning to the sound produced by the nasal exercise of the stout gentlemen when asleep.

But when the stout gentleman sleeps uninterruptedly for two hours after his usual time of rising, and hears none of the sounds that attest the beginning of another day, it becomes a matter which the historian may eminently and properly investigate.

Uncle Dan usually arose at six o'clock. It was now nearly eight. And he was still fast asleep. He had not heard the butchers' wagons — the first to disturb the gray stillness of the early morning — go racing madly after each other on their way to the markets, raising a disturbance, as they clattered past, as if all the fire engines in the city were running a race. He had not heard the early milkman, who had rung such a violent alarm on his old brass bell that it set all the dogs within three squares to barking with all their might. He had not heard the travelling tinker startle the neighborhood with his "tee-ware-t-ma-a-a-n! tee-ware-t-ma-a-a-n!" nor the charcoal man crying "Sharcoal! sharco! shawk-o! shairk-ole! shaa-wk-o-o-oal!" nor the baker yelling "Br-r-r-eadt!" until he was red in the face.

All these customary sounds made no impression upon Uncle Dan, and he slept on, snoring, as we have thrice already had the pleasure to remark, peacefully in bed.

Sleep, however, cannot last forever. And when the little, round clock above the mantel-piece marked the time, three minutes of eight, a movement indicated that Uncle Dan was on the way home from the land of dreams. In a few moments Uncle Dan opened his eyes, and perceiving how very bright the room was, immediately sat bolt upright and stared at the clock with one eye while the other was hid under the protecting shadow of the nightcap.

"Well — now!" exclaimed Uncle Dan, addressing the clock, "you really can't mean it."

The spirited little clock promptly resented the imputation, by sharply striking in a very clear, high tone, the hour — eight.

"Dear me! Dear me!" rolling out of bed with

astonishing expedition, "I've overslept myself. How very stupid! If Prudence only knew!"

And this thought so overpowered Uncle Dan that his face changed to a variety of colors in his endeavor to suppress a hearty laugh, and he said no more until he was dressed. And it must be taken as an evidence of Aunt Prudence's influence over her good-natured husband that he chuckled and choked and sneezed and coughed, and did everything but give the natural vent to his sense of the ludicrous, since there was no earthly reason why Uncle Dan should not have placed his hands on his sides and laughed with all the power of his lungs.

At length, fairly dressed, Uncle Dan turned his attention to the matter of getting his breakfast. Of the tantalizing obstacles which embarrassed Mr. Poldertot in this laudable undertaking we can say but little. They were so many and so peculiar that to record them would require more time and space than the conscientious chronicler of these pages can afford. We can only say that, in the first place, the fire would not burn. When at last a flame did feebly and obscurely flicker in one corner of the stove the water would not boil; then the stove began to smoke, and when Uncle Dan hastily opened the windows and doors the sudden draught extinguished the fire again.

At length Uncle Dan managed to warm a cup full of tea left from the evening before, and with this unsatisfactory beverage, in addition to a few pieces of bread, some dried beef, and a piece of cheese, was obliged to be satisfied. And that Uncle Dan was satisfied was amply proven by his radiant smile as he carefully folded his napkin and confidentially assured himself that his frugal meal had been a repast fit for a king. Then, arising from his chair, Uncle Dan began to busy himself in the domestic duty of washing and putting away the dishes.

Now Aunt Prudence had never kept a servant. Even if that exemplary and economical lady could have been induced to indulge in the extravagance of hired help, it may be doubted whether any servant would have been willing to work for her; since there existed a stern tradition in the neighborhood that, owing to Aunt Prudence's rigid opinions of the importance of household cleanliness, order, thrift and economy, she was capable of exhausting the strongest girl in the city by keeping her constantly employed in scrubbing the kitchen floor and the back steps, scouring the knives and forks and polishing the tea-kettle, not to mention the stew-pan and the coffee-pot.

Uncle Dan had often been impressed, amongst other things, with the great importance which Aunt Prudence attached to the proper cleansing of her table-ware; and hence Uncle Dan entered upon an elaborate preparation for the purpose of washing the few dishes he had used; a preparation that was calculated to strike with consternation and envy the hearts of all the housekeepers in the Union.

First, Uncle Dan trotted to the kitchen and brought forth an immense tin-pan two-thirds full of cold water. Having incontinently plunged all the dishes into this receptacle, Uncle Dan trotted into the kitchen again and reappeared with a bar of soap as long as his forearm, which promptly followed the dishes into the water. Then Uncle Dan carefully pinned a towel over his head — for what purpose he could not himself have explained — tied another towel before him in lieu of an apron, suspended another (secured by one corner under his collar) over his shirt bosom, appropriated a floor-cloth, evidently under the impression that it was the dish-cloth, carefully tucked up his sleeves, and, with determination and perspiration shining all over his pleasant face, prepared to execute his praiseworthy intention of rivalling Aunt Prudence in thrift and cleanliness.

But Uncle Dan's commendable endeavors were suddenly checked, even before his hand had touched the water, by a number of sharp raps delivered in quick succession against the back door, and a very shrill female voice crying, excitedly, "Mr. Poldertot! Mr. Poldertot! Mr. Poldertot!"

Uncle Dan rushed wildly to the door without waiting to divest himself of his towels, and beheld a fleshy, florid-complexioned woman, whose frowsy hair, and straggling red-calico wrapper, profusely illustrated with black dots, gave her a general appearance of having been picked up somewhere in the country by a hurricane and forcibly landed at Uncle Dan's door.

"Oh, Mr. Poldertot!" cried this disordered woman as soon as Uncle Dan made his appearance.

"Dear me! Mrs. Haddick!" ejaculated Uncle Dan.

"I've hed sech a turn!" exclaimed Mrs. Haddick, placing her hands over her left side and regarding Uncle Dan with a wildly pathetic gaze that would have frightened an infant into convulsions — "what shill I do, Mr. Poldertot? A great misfortune hes happened tu me — what shill I do?"

"You don't say! Dear me! And what is the matter?"

"Oh, Mr. Poldertot! I've just clim' up them steps tu tell you all about it."

"You don't mean to say that any of the children are sick, Mrs. Haddick?"

"No — Mr. Poldertot — it ain't thet. Ef it wus only thet, I cud stand it."

"Dear me!" cried Uncle Dan, opening his eyes wide in alarm, "the house is not on fire, is it?"

"Oh, no — no —. A bucket o' water wud cure thet." And Mrs. Haddick rolled her eyes and panted as if she might be expected to drop from excessive fear and apprehension at any moment.

"Then, my good woman," cried the now thoroughly alarmed Uncle Dan, "what on earth can be the matter?"

"It's — it's — it's the turkle-dove!"

"The turtle-dove?"

"Yes, sir: thet stupid girl o' mine — M'rier Ann — she left the cage open whilst she went fur to fill his glass with water — an' then thet turkle-dove flew out — an' he's gone — an' we cudn't kitch him — an' I've clim' up them there steps, Mr. Poldertot, fur tu tell you all about it, an' fur tu ask you, maybe now you've seed thet bird a flyin' round here some'eres. Oh, my poor turkle — my poor turkle! The cats'ill kill 'im an' then what shill I do — what shill I do?"

And then Mrs. Haddick clasped her hands and looked more wildly than ever at Uncle Dan.

Uncle Dan was immensely relieved to know that no deplorable accident had happened to any person in the neighborhood.

But he was wise enough to show nothing in his face but a serious look of sympathetic consternation.

"Dear me! Mrs. Haddick, that is too bad!" said Uncle Dan. "I have not seen the bird; but we may be able to find him yet. Did you notice the direction in which he flew?"

"Down there," said Mrs. Haddick, describing a semi-circle with her arm which included half of the horizon.

Uncle Dan looked here and there and everywhere, as far as his vision, limited by brick walls, chimney-tops and newly-washed clothes, would permit — for it was wash-day and the lines in the yards were covered with damp garments — but could see no bird.

Turning to Mrs. Haddick, Mr. Poldertot was on the point of asking another question when the whereabouts of the fugitive was revealed by a soft and melodious "Cook-er-a-coo!"

Mrs. Haddick and Uncle Dan ran to the railing of the porch and looked over.

"There he is," cried the lady, excitedly, "there he is."

There he was, sure enough, on the fence, giving vent to that peculiar sound, evidently the happiest creature in the neighborhood, and quite unmindful of a large black cat which was stealthily creeping across the yard with unmistakably murderous intentions.

Seeing the necessity for immediate action, Uncle Dan instantly ran to the stairs and began to descend with unusual haste.

Uncle Dan was eminently a creature of impulse, and as he descended hastily in his eager desire to save the bird he did not proceed with that dignity and circumspection with which a stout gentleman of his proportions should never fail to move; wherefore, as he went sailing down two steps at a time with the towel that had protected his bosom still waving over his shoulder like a flag of truce, he stepped on the edge of a bucket filled with water which some one had carelessly deposited on the stairs. The bucket capsized — so did Uncle Dan.

And away they went rolling and tumbling down together and over each other, Uncle Dan making wild lunges for the bannisters, and the bucket taking the most unheard-of liberties with his head and shoulders until they reached the foot of the stairs, where Uncle Dan was discovered by a group of horrified women, seated upon the bucket in rather a demoralized condition, it is true, but still with the air of a conqueror.

"Oh, Mr. Poldertot, are you dead?" screamed one woman as soon as she saw that he was still alive.

"He's kilt entirely," asserted a sympathetic Irish lady, with arms covered with soapsuds, notwithstanding that Uncle Dan was vigorously rubbing the back of his head.

"Oh, the poor man," cried another, "he's wet to the skin."

Uncle Dan was immediately overwhelmed by a storm of advice, respecting the proper remedies which it was of the greatest importance that he should apply to his case. They were so many — from the white of an egg to a Turkish bath — and were given with such remarkable volubility, mingled with an overpowering perfume of warm soapsuds, that Uncle Dan at length arose and raised both hands over his head and said, —

"My good women, there is really nothing the matter — nothing worth mentioning — I am all right — not hurt at all. I am ever so much obliged to you. Will you be kind enough to take this bucket away, Mrs. Callworthy? Thank you."

At this moment a piercing scream was heard from the porch above.

"Dear me!" cried Uncle Dan, "what's that?"

"Thet turkle-dove's gone!"

The shrill, high voice and the wild-looking face above the paling of the porch were unmistakably Mrs. Haddick's.

"Dear me!" exclaimed Uncle Dan, "I shouldn't wonder if that wicked cat has caught that poor little bird. I'll never forgive myself, never."

And with these words, Uncle Dan broke unceremoniously through the circle of ladies and trotted toward the place where he had last seen the lost dove. But there now was no turtle-dove to be seen.

"Where is it?" cried Uncle Dan.

"There it is — be quick!" You won't kitch him onless you hurry up," screamed Mrs. Haddick; "there's a man after 'im now on t'other side th' fence."

Thus urged, Uncle Dan excitedly turned a tub upside down, mounted it, and placing his hands on the top of the fence, pulled himself up and presented his face to the world like a suddenly arisen full moon. But the full moon promptly sunk below the horizon again in consequence of a sharp collision with another planet just rising on the other side.

"Dear me!" thought Uncle Dan, rubbing his nose and forehead, while Mrs. Callworthy and her neighbors looked at each other and smiled, "what in the world was that?"

"Mr. Poldertot!" screamed Mrs. Haddick, from above, "the man's got the turtle-dove. I see 'im kitch it. Open the gate."

"Dear me! Why didn't I think of that before?" muttered Uncle Dan. Then quickly lifting the latch and opening the gate, Uncle Dan found himself face to face with Mr. William Bromley, whose characteristic frown was at this moment severely intensified from the double fact that his forehead had received a blow, and that Mr. Ben Seldon hovered back and forth in an orbit of half a dozen yards like an erratic satellite, giving vent to such soothing reflections as occurred to him, expressive of the keenest regret and the deepest sympathy, while at the same time his eyes sparkled and his face twitched in a peculiarly spasmodic manner that clearly showed the most intense enjoyment of Mr. Bromley's misfortune.

"What!" said Uncle Dan, "Mr. Bromley! Dear me!"

"If I ever," growled Mr. Bromley, rubbing his forehead with great energy, as if he was quite determined to rub it out of existence, "If I ever get into such a scrape again — switch me."

"I'll do it, Bill," was Mr. Seldon's cheerful comment, "with pleasure."

Mr. Bromley immediately sprang toward his friendly companion, but ere he could reach the spot where Mr. Seldon had hovered, that sprightly gentleman was already several yards away — and still rapidly receding. Mr. Bromley was therefore forced to be content with a pantomimic action of his fist and head expressive of his determination to crush Mr. Seldon at the first opportunity — and then returned to Uncle Dan; whereupon, Mr. Seldon immediately resumed his orbit and hovered as before.

"Mr. Poldertot," said Mr. Bromley, after he had given the turtle-dove to Uncle Dan, who promptly handed it through the gate to its anxious owner, "there's a young lady waiting to see you."

"A young lady! Dear me! Where did she come from?"

"From our house. I brought her here."

"Well — well! And where is she now, Mr. Bromley?"

"Why, at the front door!" growled Mr. Bromley, "and she'll wonder why somebody don't open the door if you don't do it soon."

Without waiting to hear another word, Mr. Poldertot hurried through the hall to the door, and, having opened it, discovered, as Mr. Bromley had truthfully related, a young lady patiently waiting for admittance.

And if any of my dear readers had fixed their eyes upon her they would have seen a very pretty, fair, yet modest face, which blushed slightly as Uncle Dan brought his gold-rimmed spectacles to bear upon it.

CHAPTER XI.

Wherein is described the satisfactory, though wholly unexpected manner, in which Uncle Dan's advertisement was answered.

"GOOD morning, sir," said the young lady, "I would like to see Mr. Poldertot."

"You see him, ma'am," replied Uncle Dan, holding the door wide open and bowing courteously, "that is my name. Come in — come right in."

The young lady followed Uncle Dan into the parlor and took the chair which was gallantly offered, while Uncle Dan respectfully stood before her and begged to know what he could do for her.

"I must beg pardon for this early intrusion," the young lady began, "for it must seem strange to you that a stranger, and especially a lady, should call on you at this unseasonable time. But my necessities are so urgent that they must plead for me, and I hope you will accept them as my excuse." And as the young lady spoke with an engaging smile and looked at the same time pleadingly into Uncle Dan's face, there can be no doubt that soft-hearted Mr. Poldertot spoke the exact truth, so far as the feelings in his heart were concerned, when he said, —

"There is no necessity of an excuse at all, ma'am. My time is entirely at your service at any hour of the day."

Having said which, Uncle Dan, with his head bent slightly forward, his hands clasped behind his back, and a smile upon his pleasant, ruddy face, waited to hear what further the young lady might have to say. And it being quite impossible to remain at all embarrassed in the presence of such a genial gentleman, she frankly looked up into Uncle Dan's face and went on to say, "Thank you, sir. I had no intention of calling here at first, but had made up my mind to call at your place of business. But Mr. Bromley thought it would be better for me to see you here (I am stopping with Mrs. Bromley), and he was so kind as to offer to show me your house."

"Dear me! Mr. Bromley," exclaimed Uncle Dan, quite conscience-stricken. "I forgot to ask him to come in. I left him at the back-gate. My dear lady, will you please excuse me a moment until I see whether he is still waiting there?"

And Uncle Dan started for the door with self-reproach written upon his face.

"If that is all," said the young lady, smiling, "you need not leave the room, sir, for just before you opened the door I saw Mr. Seldon run by the house as fast as he could, and a moment later Mr. Bromley. Mr. Bromley does not intend to return until he has caught Mr. Seldon, even if he has to pursue him to the end of the earth."

As this picture of Mr. Bromley in hot pursuit of Mr. Seldon slowly impressed itself upon Uncle Dan's mind the lines of self-reproach gradually faded from his countenance and were succeeded by a broad, good-humored smile. And as Uncle Dan smiled and a smile also rested upon the face of the young lady it was quite a natural consequence that they should both begin to laugh heartily. And as there is no freemasonry better than a hearty laugh to put two strangers at ease in each other's presence it quite naturally followed that the last vestige of formality between Uncle Dan and the young lady was destroyed.

"And now, my dear lady," said Uncle Dan, when he had removed the tears which his laughter had produced, and had wiped his spectacles, and had drawn up his chair, and sat down, and had placed his two broad hands upon his two broad knees, "what can I do for you?"

"Mr. Poldertot," said the young lady, "I happened to notice your advertisement in the paper, and, the truth is, I am in search of employment."

"Yes," said Uncle Dan.

"And I thought that, if you had not already engaged some one for the place, perhaps I would suit you."

"Precisely," commented Uncle Dan.

"I am a stranger in the city. I came here only a few days ago, and must earn my living. If you can do anything for me I will be very thankful."

"You say you are a stranger, Miss — Miss — ah — I beg your pardon."

The young lady appeared to hesitate yet only for a moment, and then said,—

"They call me Bertha Wright."

"Ah, very good," said Uncle Dan, pleasantly nodding his head. "A very good name. Now, as to the advertisement; well, I did advertise, it is true. And I do want some one, which is equally true. But now, I suppose —merely as a matter of prudence — or rather, let me say, business habit — for really I think it is quite unnecessary — still I presume I ought to ask whether you can give me some sort of reference or recommendation, Miss Wright.

"Not that I wish to make any inquiries," hastily continued Uncle Dan, as that tender-hearted man thought that he saw some signs of distress in the lady's face, and immediately imagined that her feelings were hurt. "Not at all — but merely as a matter of form — my dear lady — merely as a matter of form."

"You are quite right," said the lady, with a sad smile, "you are quite right in asking for the reference, and I am very sorry that I cannot give you any. I am unknown here, I came from a distance. I have no friends to whom I could refer you, sir. I can only say that if you will try me, sir — you will find me faithful, and I will do the best I can."

And then the young lady took her handkerchief from her pocket and placing it to her eyes appeared to be quite overcome.

Whereupon Uncle Dan, whose gentle nature needed only this to respond completely to her appeal, threw all business tact and prudence entirely to the winds, and promised her the situation then and there; and solemnly declared that, although he might not be able to do very much for her, yet, little as it was, his help should be hers as long as she needed or desired it — and if she needed a friend or wanted assistance in any way in which it was in his power to grant it, she might rely, now and henceforth, upon the friendship of Daniel Poldertot.

And when the young lady looked up, and, with the sunniest smile imaginable, albeit tears were in her eyes, thanked Uncle Dan with the warmest words in which she could find expression for her gratitude, that kind-hearted soul felt all the more confirmed in his benevolent, although rather Quixotic resolution.

And thus did Uncle Dan render fruitless the patient waiting of that little army of mysterious people, who had first come within the range of Uncle Dan's vision in the hall of the Band of Hope — and who had that morning invaded Mr. Poldertot's queensware and crockery establishment, much to the consternation and disgust of Jimmy, who felt strongly inclined to call in the police.

CHAPTER XII.

Which begins with anticipations, continues with apprehensions, and ends with joy — all upon the part of Uncle Dan.

HEN the day set for the departure of Uncle Dan and his friends arrived, it found Mr. Poldertot busy in that most interesting of all occupations, the packing of his trunk.

Uncle Dan's travels had hitherto been confined to a distance not exceeding ten miles beyond the limits of his native city; wherefore, it is not surprising that he should regard a trip to Milton — a hundred miles away or more — as a prodigious journey, which required the greatest care and most elaborate preparation to be successfully accomplished. And in this Uncle Dan demonstrated his possession of a master mind; for, argued Mr. Poldertot, the greatest generals never proceed to action without having first carefully weighed and considered all the dangers and obstacles which they may encounter — and in accordance with this noble thought, Uncle Dan rushed wildly from room to room in a state of mingled nervousness, excitement and perspiration, gathering together a hundred different articles and piling them promiscuously into his trunk with an impartiality as to their respective qualities which was most refreshing to behold.

That Uncle Dan deliberately crammed into his trunk all sorts of articles for which he would have no earthly use, under the conviction that the country was a sort of wilderness in which it would be impossible to procure any of the common comforts of civilization, cannot be denied; and that he omitted the packing of several necessary articles is also a truth which is beyond dispute.

But as a general in the heat of battle cannot stop to deliberate upon the respective merits of his individual soldiers, but must send them, battalion by battalion, regiment by regiment, and brigade by brigade against the enemy in the hope that every man, however poor, may prove to be of some service, so Uncle Dan in the midst of his preparations for the great journey could not stop to consider such an unimportant matter as the desirability or undesirability of any particular article, but picked them all up in the greatest haste and threw them indiscriminately into the trunk, to the great amusement of Dick, who was lazily swinging back and forth in the rocking-chair, with his legs crossed, without offering to help Uncle Dan in the least. Dick apparently had the greatest respect for the principle of the right of free labor, inasmuch as he was never known to interfere with the practical operation of this principle by offering to assist any fellow-mortal in any work which that fellow-mortal seemed at all able or willing to perform. And as Uncle Dan demonstrated that he was perfectly competent to pack his trunk, Dick looked on composedly from the rocking-chair in his peculiarly indolent way, and smiled at Uncle Dan's excitement.

"Dear me," said Mr. Poldertot, stopping for a moment to remove the perspiration from his forehead, "I never had any idea that a trunk would hold so much."

Dick quietly captured a fly, held it a moment, released it again, and kept on rocking without saying a word.

"And so we are really going to the country! Well — well!" continued Uncle Dan, gravely, as if he felt a great responsibility resting upon him, "I hope we will all return safe and sound."

"No fear, sir," said Dick, reassuringly.

"Dear me, Dick." exclaimed Uncle Dan, looking at his young friend with admiration, "I wonder where you get all your coolness. You never seem to be afraid of anything. But tell me, Dick — it is always best to go prepared into these things — you know — do you think we will encounter — ah — many dangers — difficulties — anything of that kind?"

"Oh, no," said Dick, pleasantly, "nothing to speak of."

"How do we reach Milton, Dick?"

"The boat takes us to within ten miles of the village, and then we will have to ride in a wagon the rest of the way."

"Dear me!" exclaimed Uncle Dan, aghast. "Do we travel on the river?"

"Oh, yes," replied Dick.

"Well, Dick, my boy," rejoined Uncle Dan, anxiously, "had we not better go all the way by wagon?"

"That would not do," laughed Dick.

"But the boat, you know," persisted timid Uncle Dan. "We may all be drowned in the water."

"If we are drowned at all," soothingly responded Dick, "it will very probably be in the water."

This had a depressing effect upon Uncle Dan, and as he sat on the edge of the trunk and looked ruefully at a miscellaneous heap of articles lying before it waiting to be packed, Dick hastened to encourage his kind friend by adding that all boats were provided with life-preservers, and that there was no actual necessity for any person to drown unless he, or she, particularly desired it, in which case he, Dick, would gladly assist in forming a circle to see fair play.

"You don't say," said Uncle Dan, with a bewildered look; "and what are life-preservers, Dick?"

"Pieces of cork joined together — or inflated bladders, or rubber bags, which are fastened around the body under the arms and are made to keep a person afloat in the water until rescued."

"Well — well?" exclaimed Uncle Dan, in astonishment at Mr. Doolittle's knowledge. Then he glanced at his own reflection in the mirror, and at sight of his fair proportions immediately looked grave again and dubiously shook his head. From which it may be inferred that Mr. Poldertot had doubts of the wisdom of trusting those fair proportions to the support of a frail cork or a treacherous bladder.

If at this moment Uncle Dan could have been seen by his friends and acquaintances, an impression would certainly have been created that he was upon the point of taking a final departure from everything he held most dear. As to having created any such impression upon the mind of his friend Dick, nothing can be positively asserted, since that young gentleman simply continued his gentle rocking motion without comment or appearance of being affected in any manner whatever by Uncle Dan's unfeigned depression of spirits.

"You see, Dick," went on the troubled Mr. Poldertot, "if anything should happen to us on this journey I never could forgive myself — never."

"And then," proceeded Uncle Dan, seeing that Dick was not disposed to reply, "there is Prudence to be thought of. I really don't know what she will think of this excursion."

"Oh, she won't have any objections," said Dick.

"I don't know," said Uncle Dan, gravely shaking his head; and then dropping into a low tone of confidence, added, "You see, Dick, Prudence likes to be consulted about all such matters, and it is no more than right, my boy, no more than right. She is an excellent woman, a little sharp in her manner sometimes, I don't deny, but an excellent woman for all that, and I like to oblige her. And — I'll tell you something, Dick; I don't like to do anything without Prudence's approval. It does not seem right, you know — and then ——"

We shall never know with how much more domestic confidence Uncle Dan intended to entertain Dick, since at that moment there arose the loud noise of sudden warfare on the back porch, mingled with the not gentle exclamations of wrath and defiance from the unseen combatants.

"Dear me!" exclaimed Uncle Dan, "what's that?"

"Dogs," suggested Dick.

"Dogs cannot talk," replied Uncle Dan. "Dear me!" he exclaimed again, as a louder invective greeted him, succeeded by a tremendous thump against the door. "I am afraid somebody is getting hurt."

"All right," said Dick, cheerfully, "let's go and ask him how he feels."

Following his imperturbable young friend, Uncle Dan hastened to the door and looked out; and in doing so his mild blue eyes looked in horrified astonishment upon an exceedingly ragged and dirty boy engaged in a fierce struggle with an equally ragged and dirty girl. For one moment Uncle Dan stood stupefied with amazement at this unusual sight; but in the next, every impulse of his good and generous nature impelled him to rush between the struggling pair and endeavor to pull them apart. This was easier to attempt than to accomplish, and Uncle Dan found himself dragged along several feet, notwithstanding his utmost exertions, when Dick, more accustomed, doubtless, to scenes of this kind than peaceful Mr. Poldertot, leisurely sauntered forward and, grasping the boy by the collar and the girl by the arm, separated them with an unceremonious jerk and sent them flying away from each other to the ends of the porch. The boy plunged into a corner in a sadly demoralized condition, and this might have been the fate of the girl had she not fallen into the arms of a large, sunburnt, bony-armed woman who had just ascended the back stairs in a state of wild terror and alarm.

"What's the matter?" gasped Uncle Dan, panting as hard as the combatants themselves.

"What's the matter?" demanded the excited woman who held the girl.

"What's the matter?" said another woman, who was hurriedly clambering up the steps.

"What's the matter?" screamed a chorus of voices from the back-yard below.

"He's a nasty, dirty little vagabones, and I'll pull all the hair out of his head if I ketch 'im agin," sobbed the girl.

"What has he done?" demanded the woman in charge.

"What has he done?" said Uncle Dan.

"What has he done?" cried the woman on the stairs.

"What has he done?" came the faithful echo from the back-yard.

"He come up them steps, and come walkin' right over the porch where I'd been a scrubbin', an' when I told him to take his dirty feet off o' my clean porch, he wouldn't do it. An' then I ups and at 'im wid a scrubbin'-brush. Oh, you little villen! I'll give it to you, yit!"

"Dear me!" exclaimed Uncle Dan.

"Dear me!" said the staircase woman.

"Dear me!" groaned the back-yard.

"What did he come here for?" demanded the bony woman. "Didn't you ax 'im?"

"Yes, I did," sobbed the still vindictive girl, "but he didn't tell me. I guess he come here to steal something, the sneakin' little thief!"

"Thief!" said Uncle Dan, in surprise.

"Thief!" promptly reiterated the woman on the back stairs.

"Thief!" immediately roared the back-yard; and having vociferated this alarming cry with due vehemence and frequent repetition the back-yard made a sudden rush for the stairs as if a curious and very rare wild animal was at that moment presented to the public gaze.

Up to this moment the boy had stood leaning against the railing at the end of the porch, quietly sobbing and rubbing his eyes with his knuckles.

But no sooner had this serious accusation been made than he darted forward, and stopping in full view of the spectators, said, "It's a lie! I ain't a thief! I didn't come here for to steal. I'm Mr. Poldertot's boy Jim, and I come to see Mr. Poldertot."

And as he stood there with his hands clenched, his eyes flashing, and an expression of indignation upon his face, he looked, notwithstanding his ragged and dirty appearance, every inch a little hero.

Uncle Dan looked helplessly at Dick and then at Jimmy, but could make nothing of it. But Dick, who was never known to be overcome by surprise, said, "Say, Jim, you're a nice boy to come prize-fighting a girl at your master's door."

"I didn't come for to fight," said Jimmy, indignantly, "I come to see Mr. Poldertot. I bring him a 'spatch."

"Ah!" remarked Dick.

Which was all that Dick said. But as he left the wall against which he had been lazily leaning, and grasping Mr. Poldertot's arm as well as Jimmy's, gently pushed them into the house, turned in the doorway, bowed gravely and politely to the promiscuous audience, and then quietly shut the door in their faces, it was doubtless quite unnecessary for him to say another word.

"If any one had asked me," said Uncle Dan, with a slow meditative utterance, "who is the last person whom I expected to honor me with a visit I should have been strongly tempted to answer 'Jimmy Brankey.' I would, indeed."

Jimmy promptly answered "Yes'r," and looked at the floor.

"You see, Jimmy," observed Uncle Dan, "I can't for the life of me imagine what has brought you here."

"Yes'r," responded Jimmy as before.

"For, don't you see," continued Uncle Dan, in argumentative strain, as if Jimmy had just strenuously denied a proposition which had been put forth and plainly needed to be argued into conviction, "that it stands to reason that I would suppose that you were at present in the store with Miss Wright."

"It was her sent me for to come up here, sir," said Jimmy.

"Dear me! you don't say so!"

"Yes'r."

"Well — well; and what did she send you for?"

Without immediately replying, Jimmy began an earnest search for the pocket in the right side of his garments, and as the opening to this receptacle lay hidden among many other openings, owing to the chronic state of ventilation in which Jimmy's clothes existed, it was some time before he could make way through these peculiar pitfalls and insert his hand into the depository of his treasure; and when he had successfully accomplished this feat it was almost as hard to release it again owing to a settled determination upon the part of the pocket to cling to its owner's hand, and turn inside out rather than let go.

After a brave struggle Jimmy succeeded in producing an envelope, on the lower left-hand corner of which was written a number.

"Dear me!" exclaimed Uncle Dan, as he received the message from the boy, while his face paled, "a telegram!"

The wires were not an institution for which Uncle Dan had ever had much use, such messages as he had received relating mainly to the severe illness or sudden death of a near relative or friend. Wherefore it is not astonishing that Uncle Dan held the dreaded envelope off at arm's length and surveyed it with a glance of dire dismay.

"Dear me! Dear me!" said the poor gentleman, "I have a brother out West. I wonder whether he's dead."

Dick, tilted back in a chair, with his feet elegantly supported by another, looked as if the death of a whole army of relations would not affect him in the least.

"Or perhaps it is one of my sisters," groaned Mr. Poldertot, "there is one in New York, and one in Alabama."

Then Uncle Dan examined the envelope carefully, turned it over and over, glanced fearfully at the corners as if the ghost of the departed might suddenly issue therefrom, and finding no comfort in this examination, with a long drawn sigh, continued, "Or it may be Aunt Prudence!" At this thought a deeper pallor overspread his usually ruddy face, and Uncle Dan sank into a chair, a most forlorn and miserable man.

"Dick," he managed to utter, in a faint tone.

"Here!" promptly replied Dick, returning the coffee-pot, which had just been artistically balanced above his nose, to the table, "always on hand, sir, — like a sore thumb."

"I wish I knew what this is about."

"Just so," said Dick.

"If anything has happened to Prudence, I can never forgive myself — never in the world."

It was like Uncle Dan to blame himself first and always for any harm or trouble, real or fancied, that overtook Aunt Prudence.

"Well, sir," said Dick, mildly, and without the least appearance of interest in the whole matter, "what do you expect to do with that dispatch?"

"I really don't know, Dick. What would you do?"

"Read it," said Dick. And then Dick yawned.

"Dear me! Dear me! I had not thought of that. How stupid!"

With unsteady hands Uncle Dan took his spectacles from his pocket, nervously opened them and slowly put them upon his nose. Then reluctantly and with trembling fingers he drew forth the message from its covering and held it out, first with the blank side and then with the written side held upside down before him. But at length he held it in proper position, and with a sinking heart began to read.

It is safe to say, however, that the sinking heart did not sink very far. For no sooner had Uncle Dan read the telegram than he bounced to his feet so suddenly that the spectacles flew from his nose and landed on the stove, and with a beaming face, whose color was carmine in comparison with its recent paleness, uttered a "hurrah!" that a sand-lot Californian might have envied, and began to dance about the room in such a wild and undignified manner that Jimmy's eyes and mouth, like the boundless prairies of the West, were "open," and even Dick removed his feet from the chair before him and began to softly whistle his unusual interest in these proceedings.

"Hurrah! Hurrah! Hurrah!" cried Uncle Dan, capering wildly about and waving the dispatch triumphantly, as a sailor might do who has captured the enemy's pennant.

"Go it," said Dick, encouragingly, "go it, Uncle Dan, while you're young."

"Dick," laughed the overjoyed Mr. Poldertot, executing a peculiar movement with his feet, which he could not have done again to save his life, "it's all settled."

"What is all settled?" inquired Dick.

"The trip to the country," replied Uncle Dan.

"How is it settled?" demanded Dick.

"Read that," said Uncle Dan.

Dick took the message from Uncle Dan and read it. It was brief and to the point:—

"DANIEL POLDERTOT. — Don't pack your trunk. Milton folks all down sick. Fever and ague. Hold on. BOB."

"Of course," said Uncle Dan, as soon as he had recovered his composure, "I am sorry that our friends are sick and also sorry that you will miss your pleasure; but I dreaded the travelling by river Dick, I did, indeed."

CHAPTER XIII.

Mr. Poldertot and his friends meet in order to leave the city together. — A very nice young lady. — The arrival of Mr. Krowps.

FOR several days the thought that his young friends, Dick, Harry and Bob, had been disappointed in thus having their visit to Milton indefinitely postponed troubled Uncle Dan exceedingly, and occasioned the wildest and most impracticable projects in that good gentleman's mind for the comfort and pleasure of the young men. Fortunately for his own peace of mind, the necessity of deciding the momentous question as to where their summer holiday should be spent — for that they were to have a holiday was a fixed determination in Uncle Dan's mind — was removed by the receipt of an urgent invitation from "Sister Sarah," requesting "Uncle Dan and friends" to pay her a visit during Aunt Prudence's stay: which invitation being supplemented by a short note from his beloved wife, to the effect that he had better come without any "dilly-dallying," relieved Uncle Dan's mind immensely and settled the whole matter in the neatest and most satisfactory manner possible.

"Brother John will call for you with the wagon on Wednesday morning; so be sure to be ready and don't keep him waiting," was the characteristic closing paragraph of Aunt Prudence's note.

Consequently, precisely a week and a day after the date of the events narrated in the last chapter Uncle Dan was again busily engaged in packing his trunk, very much in the same excited manner as before, and also, as before, in the company of his friend Mr. Richard Doolittle.

"Well, well—" said Uncle Dan, working away over his trunk with the interest of a boy in the occupation of making a kite, "and so we are going to the country after all, eh, Dick?"

"Seems so," said Dick from the sofa, where he lay at full length with a satchel by his side and a magazine elevated above his nose.

"And without the necessity of travelling on a boat," continued Uncle Dan, in a pleased tone, "that is the best of it. No bladders or rubber bags or pieces of cork to paddle around in the water with." (Uncle Dan mentioned these contrivances with a slight expression of disgust, as if a trip on the river would necessarily involve a tumble into the water under the auspices of life-preservers, which he evidently regarded as a frail and unsatisfactory institution.) "But now we'll have a nice ride, and after that, the jolliest time — just the jolliest time, my boy!"

At this point Uncle Dan found it necessary to turn his face, beaming with smiles, toward Dick, and rub his hands in quiet enjoyment.

"And everything has happened so nicely;" continued Uncle Dan, "if Sarah had invited me when Aunt Prudence went I could not have gone, you know. But now with Miss Wright in the store, I feel free to make a perfect rover of myself, a perfect rover, Dick."

It would have done any one good to have seen gentle Uncle Dan at this moment as he plunged his hands into his pockets by way of emphasis and stood with his feet wide apart, looking down at Dick, while smiles and perspiration covered his round, ruddy face.

"Ah," said Dick, from under the magazine, "how do you like Miss Wright?"

"Dick," said Uncle Dan, with great emphasis, "she is worth her weight in gold — yes, sir, in — in diamonds!"

"Good!" commented Dick.

"She is," reasserted Uncle Dan, "worth her weight in diamonds and twice over at that. Why, she is the best, handiest, politest, smartest, most tractable young woman it has ever been my pleasure to know. Really she is a treasure, Dick, and I must introduce you to her."

"Oh," said Dick calmly, "I have met her already."

"Indeed!" said Uncle Dan. "Well, then you know that she is a charming young lady. There is a little mystery connected with her former life, for she will not tell where she came from. But she works faithfully. Why, dear me, she mastered all the details of the business in a week, and she knows as much about it now as I do."

"So," said Dick, quietly turning a page of the magazine, "you don't know where she came from?"

"No," replied Uncle Dan, "and Mrs. Bromley — you know she is stopping with the Bromleys for the present — knows no more about her than I do."

"Not that I made any inquiries about her," Uncle Dan hastened to add, "but the good woman met me on the street and told me voluntarily — quite voluntarily, Dick."

"You did not ask her for any recommendation, then?" inquired Dick.

"Dear me! Yes," said Uncle Dan. "But she had no references. She is all right."

"And you are not afraid to trust her," pursued Dick, "while you are gone?"

"Oh, Dick, my dear boy? Trust her. She is so faithful — and Jimmy is there."

Dick smiled peculiarly behind his magazine and said no more.

And Uncle Dan, suddenly seized with a strong conviction that Brother John's wagon would immediately make its appearance and depart without him, like a railroad train, — unless he was prepared to travel at a moment's notice, again went wildly to work putting numerous unnecessary articles into his trunk in a promiscuous and most unreasonable manner. And when it is stated that Uncle Dan carefully placed a bar of soap in close proximity to a bundle of clean shirts, and put a mirror on the soap, a pair of boots on the mirror, some towels on the boots, and a box of blacking and a paper of pins on the towels, the reader will have a faint idea of the able manner in which Mr. Poldertot continued his elaborate preparations for the journey.

At last the preparations were completed, the trunk was strapped and locked and Uncle Dan sat upon it with a glossy silk-hat beside him. And why Uncle Dan should have procured this expensive and extremely uncomfortable covering for his head, this being an entirely new departure, involving for this good man a great responsibility, seeing that the care of it would be a burden upon his mind as well as a torture to his head, passeth the comprehension of the perplexed historian.

Uncle Dan sat upon his trunk anxiously awaiting the arrival of his friends, Mr. Sturdy and Mr. Cribbler, as also Brother John and the wagon. He was waiting with expectation tempered with impatience, and he had even begun to express his anxiety by saying,—

"Dear me! Where can Bob and Harry be? I do hope they won't disappoint us," when the sound of approaching footsteps was heard in the hall; and a moment later Mr. Sturdy and Mr. Cribbler presented themselves.

"Dear me! Here you are at last," exclaimed Mr. Poldertot, "come in, come in."

The invitation was entirely unnecessary since Mr. Sturdy immediately entered the room before Mr. Poldertot had had time to say a word, and Mr. Cribbler, as might have been expected, promptly followed.

No sooner had Mr. Sturdy entered the room than he espied his friend Mr. Doolittle reclining upon the sofa.

"Dick," observed little Bob, appropriating a chair and sitting down beside his prostrate friend, "did it ever occur to you that you are unconscionably lazy?"

Dick looked up at Bob, slowly closed one eye, and then assumed an expression which was so perfectly blank that it was no expression at all.

"You are complimentary, Bob," said Harry.

"So I am," said Bob, "it's a compliment to him to call him lazy — it's worse — it's gross flattery."

"Only," put in Uncle Dan, gently, "you must not be so harsh in your criticisms."

"Harsh!" cried Bob, in order to check off each sentence with a swift downward motion, as was his wont when he desired to be more than usually impressive, "harsh! Why, Uncle Dan, I am not half harsh enough."

"How is the picture of Napoleon getting on?" inquired Uncle Dan, by way of changing the subject.

"Capitally!" said Bob, with enthusiasm, "swimmingly! And Harry's book is growing. It is a great undertaking. Now, Harry, not a word from you. You're always crying down your own wares. But I know what they are. Just wait. When that book is completed — and when that picture is done — there will be a sensation : then this lazy fellow will hide his head. He'll feel as small as a nickel with a hole in it. Just wait till we get the work done."

"And when you do," said Dick, rising and

favoring Bob with a comical glance from one eye, "I'll give you a lock of my gray hair and let you marry one of my grand-daughters."

The insinuation conveyed in these words was such that Bob ran his fingers excitedly through his hair, and he would certainly have demolished his tall friend then and there, in his usual wordy fashion, had not Uncle Dan rushed noisily to the window upon hearing the sound of wagon wheels.

And as their worthy leader had no sooner thrust his head out of the window than he began to frantically wave his arms and to cry,—

"Ho, Krowps! Here you are! This way — two doors further. Glad to see you — glad to see you, Brother John. Come right in," they promptly followed their illustrious leader's example and thrust their heads out of the other in excusable haste and excitement. And directing their glances toward the street beheld a square, springless, heavy, country wagon to which was attached a horse and a mule. The driver, who had descended from the wagon, and was now securing his ill-assorted team to a small maple-tree with a piece of rope, was a muscular, sunburnt, red-bearded man, whose attire consisted of a slouch hat, a coarse woollen shirt (without a collar), jeans trousers, and extraordinarily large boots (which looked with their innumerable wrinkles as hard and unyielding as wood), all of a uniformly rusty yellow-clay color.

"Say, Harry," said Bob, while a look of consternation spread over his face.

"What?" said Harry, with an equally uncomfortable expression.

"Are we going to ride in that?"

"It looks like it."

An expression of the keenest disgust passed over Bob's face.

"Suppose somebody we know sees us."

Harry sighed.

Unconscious of the feelings of these young gentlemen, the farmer clambered slowly and clumsily up the stairs with a noise as if a platoon of soldiers was advancing.

Then Uncle Dan looked at Bob and smiled, and Bob looked at Harry and groaned, and Harry looked at Dick and sighed. But Dick looked at neither one nor the other, and without the slightest expression of interest in anything that was going on around, gazed abstractedly out of the window

CHAPTER XIV.

Mr. Krowps converses sociably, and expatiates upon the virtues of tooth-powders.

OH, how d'you do? All well, Dan'l? Got your traps all ready. Them thar's the boys, I s'pose. Sarvice, gentlemen. Glad to see you. All ready, as I see. Ever ready — ever right," said Mr. Krowps, as soon as he had presented his sun-reddened face in the doorway. Then Mr. Krowps advanced across the room in a friendly rush of familiarity, and shook hands all around without waiting for the formality of an introduction. Having completed this polite exercise, Mr. Krowps made so bold as to sit down on Uncle Dan's trunk, and as Uncle Dan's new silk-hat happened to be in the way, that expensive article received a crushing from which it never wholly recovered.

"Beg pardon — beg pardon," stammered Brother John, pulling the hat from under him and smoothing out the wrinkles with his horny hand, meanwhile rubbing in the wrong direction and giving the unfortunate article the appearance of having been out on a late convivial tour, "beg pardon — beg pardon."

"Oh, it is nothing," said Uncle Dan, affecting to make light of it and taking the hat from his confused relative, — "it does not matter. Sit down, Brother John, sit down, and tell us how you left all the folks. All well, I hope."

"Oh, yes — oh, yes," said Mr. Krowps, "all well — fust rate — well an' hearty; that is to say, pooty well, considerin'. Joel's had a tech o' the fever'n'ager, an' he ain't quite shet of it yet; Ca'line's rheumatiz has been a leetle wus, but now it's a leetle better, tho' she ain't nothin' to brag on yet; the youngest hes had a spell o' sickness, an' the old 'ooman's got the toothache, but otherwise we're all right. Health couldn't be better."

Dick's face had certainly lengthened, while Bob's and Harry's faces had correspondingly brightened, for they anticipated Uncle Dan's saying, as he did:

"Dear me, I am so sorry to hear that you have had so much sickness. I am sure we will be only a burden to you and Sister Sarah if we visit you at present. It was very kind of you to come, Brother John, but I think it will be better to postpone our visit until some other time."

"No, sir — no, sir. Couldn't think of it. Not

at all. Nothin's the matter. We're all right. The old 'ooman, ses she to me, 'be sure you bring Dan'l.' 'Yes,' ses I, 'all right. I'll hev him h'yer ef I hev to drag him out o' the house.' 'An' don't forgit the tooth-powder,' ses she. 'No,' ses I, 'I won't,' ses I. 'It's the best thing for the toothache ever you seed,' ses she. 'Ol' Deacon Powers' wife told me,' ses she, 'thet her mother's father onct knew a man whose daughter's husband heard his cousin's nephew tell another man as thet man knew a woman onct who tried it, an' three days arterward she had a bran' new set o' teeth! Don't believe it myself,' ses she, 'but thur must be some truth in't, an' I've got a powerful jumpin' tooth; so don't forgit the tooth-powder,' ses she. 'No,' ses I. 'Nor Daniel,' ses she. 'No,' ses I. 'Nor the young men,' ses she. 'No,' ses I. An' so I druv away. My wife's a good 'ooman, she is — a mite bit given to gab, mebbe, but I don't mind it, an' if I don't, who shell?"

"No one, of course," said Uncle Dan.

"Certainly not," said Bob.

"Did Aunt Prudence send no message?" inquired Harry.

"Well," said the farmer, scratching his head, meditatively, "she said as how she'd expected Dan'l 'd be kinder keerful to shet up the house an' be sure to lock the doors an' not to keep me waitin' longer'n wuz necessary." And looking upon this gentle admonition in the light of an excellent joke, Farmer Krowps felt obliged to open a rather huge mouth and entertain the company with an explosive and not very gentle guffaw.

Uncle Dan smiled and nodded to Robert and Richard and Harry as if to say, "Isn't she an admirable woman?"

"An' thet reminds me," said Mr. Krowps rising, "thet we'd better be startin' ef we want to get home afore dark. So, gentlemen, ef you've all got your traps ready, jest heave 'em into the wagon an' les' be a goin' along."

"Don't hurry," said Uncle Dan, "stop and have a cup of tea and a bite of something."

"No, Dan'l," said Brother John, decidedly, "we hain't got no time to waste over victuals, 'sides th' old 'ooman's goin' to hev a stavin' good supper for us, an' I don't want to spile my appetite."

Having thus delivered himself, Brother John resolutely shouldered Uncle Dan's trunk, notwithstanding its owner's earnest offers of assistance, and thus encumbered, resolutely led the way to the wagon. Uncle Dan followed, still loudly protesting his desire to assist in carrying the baggage, and declaring that it was a shame to allow Farmer Krowps to act as porter.

Wherefore there remained nothing for the young men to do but to grasp their satchels, carefully close the windows and lock the doors (which Uncle Dan had forgotten to do), and follow their illustrious leader to the pavement. And in a few moments our heroes were being jolted slowly out of the city in the direction of the setting sun.

CHAPTER XV.

Which records not only the extremely novel and highly interesting exercises of Uncle Dan and his companions, but also the gloomy political reflections of the astute Mr. Krowps.

TO the immense relief of Mr. Sturdy and Mr. Cribbler, they succeeded in passing the city limits without meeting any of their friends or acquaintances; for, not only was the wagon one of the rustiest of rural vehicles, but it appeared to have been constructed with the fiendish design of jolting the life out of every person who had the temerity to ride on its rough board seats. It is safe to presume that if Bob and Harry had possessed the faintest idea of the character of the conveyance in which they were destined to journey they would politely have declined Uncle Dan's invitation as soon as received. As the wagon lumbered along, making a clattering noise, our four inexperienced travellers bounced up and down in the most extraordinary manner, and came so frequently and violently in contact with the rough planks upon which they were trying to sit, that the tears came into their eyes, while they gave vent to exclamations that were as earnest as they were loud and unpremeditated. Added to this, the seats were loose and kept constantly slipping down, to the great disgust of the travellers who were thereby precipitated to the bottom of the wagon.

"Oh — ah! Dear me!" exclaimed Uncle Dan, as he came down with a dull thud, "how very rough this road is!"

"It's nothin' when you get used to it," consolingly remarked Farmer Krowps.

"Well, if there is much of this kind, I don't want to get used to it — oh, my!" and Bob completed his sentence by going over backwards into Dick's lap.

"Look!" said Harry, rising tremblingly to his feet, "see that beautiful scene. Isn't it fine?"

Whereupon the attention of his companions was immediately attracted — not by the beauty of the scenery — but by the spectacle of Mr. Harry Cribbler diving wildly under Uncle Dan, owing to one of the front wheels of the wagon having come in contact with a stone.

As for Dick, he was perched upon the top of Uncle Dan's trunk, to which the jolting, springless wagon contributed a peculiar, rocking, jerky

Uncle Dan and his friends go into the country.—Page 176.

motion, and performed such intricate and wonderful evolutions in the endeavor to keep his seat and prevent being thrown over the tail-board into the road, that if Mr. Barnum had seen him he would have promptly engaged him and the whole outfit at an enormous salary to appear nightly before appreciative and enthusiastic audiences.

In this manner they travelled for some distance, passing numerous vehicles of many descriptions, from skeleton hay-wagons to the country gentleman's carriage, but so occupied were they with their own affairs that they could not afterward have described a single person whom they had then seen on the road. Further than an occasional assurance that they would be "off er this hyer macker-demized road pooty soon an' then trav'lin' 'll be easier," the farmer carried on but little conversation with his friends, owing to an obstinate tendency on the part of the horse to turn to the left, while the mule manifested an equally determined disposition to turn to the right, which necessitated continued pullings and jerkings of the reins to keep the animals on the right path.

When they had travelled in this manner a distance of nearly ten miles, the farmer suddenly pulled the left rein, shifting his seat a little with the air of a man to whom the worst part of a job is over, and lighting a match on his knee, lit his pipe with the match, and began to smoke in a comfortable way.

"Halloa!" said Bob, "this is a new road."

"That's so," said Harry.

"Rides easier, too," said Uncle Dan, much pleased; "what road is this, Brother John?"

"Well," said Brother John, taking the pipe from his mouth with his thumb and forefinger, "that depends. Some folks calls it the state road — some calls it the country road — some calls it the Kirkwood road — some calls it the Big Bend. As for me, I calls it the road home when I'm a goin' home, an' the road to town when I goes to town." And having thus delivered himself, for Uncle Dan's edification, he replaced the pipe — a short black one — and smoked away vigorously.

After a few moments of silence the farmer again spoke, with emphatic decision, —

"I don't like macker-demized roads."

"Don't you?" said Uncle Dan, with surprise. "Why, I thought a good macadamized road is an excellent highway. Why don't you like them?"

"Wal!" said the farmer, "in the fust place they're hard on cattle — hosses an mules included — an' then again they costs a heap o' money, an' we farmers have got to pay for it. An' thur ain't no use in 'em anyway. Why, ef I had my sayso, I'd hev every one o' them stones tooken up an' hev the good old-fashioned clay roads all over the kentry. But it's this h'yur guv'ment that's a doin' of it all. Ever since them thar Radikel fellers hev come into power the poor man's ground into the dust an' stands no show. An' what's the kentry a comin' to? Why, this h'yur guv'ment's a convartin' this glorious kentry into a—into—a—" Here he paused in want of a suitable word; but only for a few moments; and then concluded grandly—"into a—into a fretful porkipine! Yes, sir," said Mr. Krowps, repeating this eloquent sentence with great unction, "they're a convartin' it into a fretful porkipine!"

And having thus declared his sentiments, Brother John's lips closed over his pipe and he fell to smoking again, puffing out the smoke at long and regular intervals with the sober and exalted expression of a man who feels that he has just delivered himself of one of the profoundest sentiments that any statesman could have uttered.

Uncle Dan smiled and made no reply. Bob and Harry looked at each other as if their feelings were too strong for utterance. And Dick included them all in one comprehensive wink and then looked blandly inexpressive for the rest of the journey.

They rode on in comparative silence for fifteen minutes longer, when the farmer went through the extraordinary performance of putting his feet against the dashboard, reclining backward until he occupied an almost horizontal position, squaring his elbows, whereby one of them came into painful contact with Uncle Dan's side, and shouting "Whoa!" with all his might.

The assorted team accordingly "whoa'd," and came to a stand still; and the farmer with a "Here we are!" descended to the ground. Peering through the gathering darkness—for it had been growing dark for some time—Uncle Dan could just see the dim outlines of a house in a field, some distance from the road, and a group of people gathered before it. Their journey was ended. They had reached their destination. And, clambering out of the wagon, they followed Brother John along a well-worn footpath toward the little group which was already approaching to welcome and receive them.

CHAPTER XVI.

A warm welcome.—The meeting of Uncle Dan and Aunt Prudence.

OUR travellers received a warm welcome, especially from Sister Sarah, a lady who remarkably resembled Aunt Prudence, and who presented a picturesque appearance owing to a broad strip of red flannel which encircled her face.

Mr. John Krowps waived the formality of an introduction of each member of his family, and simply saying, "My wife, gentlemen," considered his duty in that direction done. However, as Brother John's family were evidently possessed of a determination to make the travellers feel at home as soon as possible, and as Uncle Dan never permitted the omission of a formality to stand in the way of better acquaintance, they were all soon on excellent terms and needed no extended or particular introduction.

"Now, come right into the house," said Sister Sarah, speaking in a muffled tone, owing to the toothache and the red flannel, "for the night air isn't good for city-bred folks. Prudence caught a bad cold the first night she came out, 'cause she wasn't used to it."

"Dear me!" said Uncle Dan, in a tone of deep contrition, "where is Prudence? I declare, I forgot all about her."

"She's in the house," said Sister Sarah, "she don't venture out after dark."

"Dear me!" said Uncle Dan. And he said no more until he stood in the doorway and saw Aunt Prudence waiting for him in the room.

Then he said, "Ah, Prudence, my dear!" and hurried toward her and folded her in his arms and kissed her as tenderly as if she were a blooming bride and he had but just led her from the altar.

It was a pleasant sight and caused Bob, Dick, and Harry to hold their kind-hearted leader in greater esteem than ever before.

"Now, that will do," said Aunt Prudence, sharply, but she looked pleased, nevertheless — "don't act as silly as a school-boy. Before company, too! Young gentlemen, how do you do? I am glad to see you. I hope you have come to behave yourselves."

Such was Aunt Prudence's characteristic greeting.

"I hope so," said Harry.

"Of course we have — not a doubt about it, Aunt Prudence," said Bob, with his usual prompt decision.

Dick said nothing.

From a wide hall their hostess had led them into the best room, and Sister Sarah hastened away to prepare the supper with the assistance of her daughters Caroline, and Mary.

The house was a large, old-fashioned country-house, of which the principal portion had originally been built of logs. But by dint of industry, patience, and careful husbanding of his resources, Brother John had succeeded in somewhat improving upon this pioneer style of architecture. The exterior of the house was now covered with clapboards, and the wall of the interior with pine boards and wall-paper. Large open fire-places — mats instead of carpets on the floors — guns and a large clock on the walls — and severely plain household furniture were the home features of Brother John's residence.

Brother John's family consisted of himself and his good wife Sarah; a son Joel, aged twenty-four, another son, John, aged twenty-one — two daughters, Caroline and Mary, aged respectively nineteen and ten; and a son, Hank, aged eight.

As the travellers were supposed to be very tired, notwithstanding Uncle Dan's earnest assurance that they were not fatigued in the least, but were, on the contrary, "as fresh as a lark," they were shown to their rooms immediately after supper and advised to take a good long nap, in order to prepare for a fine day's sport upon the morrow. Owing to limited sleeping accommodations it was necessary for Bob, Dick and Harry to occupy a bed together.

After considerable good-humored scuffling and pinching and pushing, two or three pitched battles with pillows in the dark, and a great deal of suppressed laughter, which broke out now and then into such a sudden and explosive cachinnation that Uncle Dan, in the next room, felt called upon to hammer on the wall with his hand, as a gentle reminder that silence would be more agreeable to their neighbors, and more appropriate under the circumstances, at any rate, Bob and Harry fell asleep.

But Dick could not sink into slumber so soon. In the first place, because it was still early — only half-past eight o'clock, — and in the city Dick seldom touched his pillow before eleven ; and in the second place, because he felt a burning desire to explore the house and the neighborhood, and, as this was impracticable, he was obliged to lie awake thinking about it until after midnight, when he fell into a fitful, restless sleep, disturbed by his own uneasy dreams and the sonorous nasal sound with which Uncle Dan testified to the peacefulness of his unbroken slumbers.

CHAPTER XVII.

The painful result of Mr. Doolittle's pugilistic dreams, and Mr. Poldertot's eloquent plea in behalf of the innocent creatures of the forest.

A VIOLENT shaking administered to Mr. Dick Doolittle upon the morning after his arrival in the country awoke him from his sleep. Now, it happened that a moment before our friend, Mr. Doolittle, was thus rudely awakened he had been troubled with dreams of an uncomfortable nature, in which certain belligerent parties were determined to summarily chastise him, while he was just as determined to resist any such indignity to the full extent of his power; wherefore, when he was roughly pushed back and forth in his bed, the impression that the aforesaid belligerent parties had seized and were preparing to execute dire vengeance upon him so took possession of his mind that he doubled up his right hand and violently propelled it from him.

In the next moment Dick was sitting on the edge of the bed, with his eyes wide open, staring in a half-sleepy and wholly bewildered manner at a gentleman who was seated on the floor, and who was rocking back and forth and groaning with pain, while he held both his hands tightly clasped against his left eye.

"Halloa!" said Dick, as soon as he was wide awake enough to say anything.

"Oh! Oh! Oh!" groaned the floored gentleman,

"Is that you, John?" inquired Dick, trying to rub the sleep out of his eyes with the back of his hand. "What's the matter?"

"Oh, my eye! Oh! Oh!"

"What ails you? Who struck you?"

"You did!"

"I!"

Then Dick attempted to whistle his astonishment, but failing, he devoted another stare to the gentleman before him and said, "How?"

"Why," said Mr. John Krowps, Jr., in an injured tone, and looking indignantly at Dick with his right eye, "I shook you to make you get up an' you let drive with your fist an' knocked me down."

Now, if it had been Uncle Dan, or even Bob or Harry, who had thus assaulted a friend — even in sleep — they would, upon being informed of the fact, have immediately been overwhelmed with confusion and instantly begun to beg a thousand pardons. But Dick simply locked his fingers around one of his knees and coolly asked, "Was it a square blow?"

"You'd thought it was a square blow, and a round blow, too, if you'd got it in the eye the way I did," grumbled John, rising to his feet and keeping the injured optic covered with one hand.

"John," said Dick, generously, "I'm sorry."

"Yes, I guess so," retorted John, gloomily, "but you won't catch me a waking of you again. Not by a long shot."

"Oh — waking me!" exclaimed Dick, looking around. "Must be so. What time is it? Where are Sturdy and Cribbler?"

"They've been down stairs these two hours," said John, becoming a little friendlier, as the pain departed, "and I was sent up to get you out of bed. Breakfast's ready."

A wholesome respect kept him at a distance from Mr. Doolittle, who, as soon as the word "breakfast" was pronounced, began to dress himself with great expedition.

"Come on," said John, and then he disappeared.

When Dick reached the dining-room, he found the family and his particular friend waiting for him. A chorus of exclamations greeted his appearance.

"Why, Dick," exclaimed Uncle Dan, — "this is

a bad beginning. You have lost a splendid sunrise."

"And a glorious hunt for eggs," said Harry, his face flushed with enthusiasm and early morning exposure, to which he was not accustomed, "besides a glass of fresh milk."

"Dick always was a lazy fellow — always said so — now you know it," was Bob's comment.

"Hain't larn't country hours yit," observed Mr. Krowps, "but that'll come bimeby, eh, Dick?"

"Well — well," said Sister Sarah, smiling pleasantly (owing partially to the excellent effect of the tooth-powders,) "he was tired last night. He'll do better to-morrow."

"No — no, he won't," retorted Bob, with a toss of his bushy head — "I know him — it's in him — he's lazy — to the backbone."

Dick, seated quietly in his chair, with his elbow on the window-sill, made no reply, but smiled in his peculiar manner as if he felt perfectly competent to demolish them all with a word if he only felt so disposed.

"Come!" said Aunt Prudence, sharply, "let him alone. Breakfast is ready — and waiting. Coffee is getting cold. Come to the table — every one."

In obedience to this peremptory summons, the

little company gathered around the table and took their seats, Uncle Dan at its head as the honored guest.

"Dad," said Joel, after grace had been said, "I'm goin' huntin' to-day."

"Huntin'!" exclaimed the elder Mr. Krowps, with his fork suspended above a savory piece of bacon, "whatever put that into your head?"

"I don' know," said his son frankly, putting a slice of bread to his mouth. And when he removed it again it had sensibly diminished.

"Huntin'!" said Mr. Krowps again in a state of astonishment — "h'yur's that ten-acre patch to cut, an' the bay hoss to take down to the blacksmith: — I'd like to know what you want to go huntin' for to-day."

Then Mr. Krowps made a ferocious charge upon the bacon, and captured it and began without further hesitation to demolish it.

"Well," said Joel, speaking with some difficulty, owing to a mouthful of bread and ham — "I han't had no holiday sence last winter an' I'll be switched ef I work to-day. I'm goin' huntin'."

"Dear me!" said Uncle Dan, presenting a troubled face, "I hope you won't go, Joel."

Joel favored Uncle Dan with a look of some surprise.

"Not that I wish to prevent you from having a holiday, Joel. That is all right and proper, and I'm sure I, for one, will ask Brother John to let you off for one day, at least. But I don't see the profit or the pleasure in hunting down the innocent and harmless creatures of the forest."

"Well, I decleer!" observed Mr. Krowps, with considerable force, "that's the fust time I ever heard a man talk like that."

"There they are," pursued Uncle Dan, warming with his subject, and stretching his arm across the table, "there they are placed by a merciful Creator, far from the haunts of man, in the leafy shadows of the woods in the possession of life and happiness. Here are we, endowed with superior abilities, and having everything about us that is necessary to our daily comfort, peace and happiness, plotting how we may add a little more excitement to our lives by inflicting upon these playful, helpless denizens of the woods unnecessary pain and cruel death. Oh, it can't be right, my friends, it can't be right."

However, notwithstanding Uncle Dan's eloquence upon the subject, it was arranged that a hunting expedition should take place, but expressly upon this condition;—that only so much game should be brought home as could be used, and that no firing at birds or animals simply "for fun" should be permitted. Upon these conditions Uncle Dan gave his reluctant consent and even agreed to carry a gun himself.

But that good man chuckled considerably as he quietly determined to aim in such a scientific manner that the object fired at would be absolutely as safe as if it were a thousand miles away. At the same time Uncle Dan made up his mind to make as much noise as possible in passing through the woods in order to frighten away the threatened dwellers of the forest and thus to limit the destruction of life considerably.

And how the kind-hearted Mr. Poldertot carried out these determinations the next chapter shall definitely and particularly state.

CHAPTER XVIII.

How the visitors hunted. — Mr. Sturdy's vainglorious boasting and his ignominious failure. — The fruitlessness of Uncle Dan's benevolent intentions and his consequent grief.

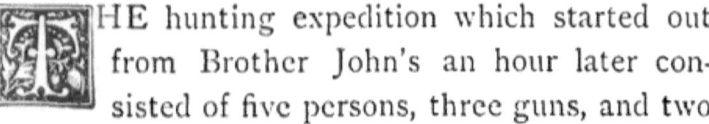HE hunting expedition which started out from Brother John's an hour later consisted of five persons, three guns, and two game-bags; the guns being in the possession of Uncle Dan, Dick and Joel, and the game-bags in charge of Bob and Harry; this being merely a temporary arrangement, as Mr. Sturdy and Mr. Cribbler expected to do their share of the shooting as well as the other intrepid marksmen.

Indeed, Bob boasted so loudly of his ability as a sharp-shooter that he readily induced the belief that the empty game-bag he carried would be returned full to the top with game brought down by his skilful hand alone; and talked with such great assurance of the certainty of his "hitting the bull's eye every time," that he was kindly warned by Mr. Krowps to confine his efforts to wild game, and not to fire promiscuously at the cattle and domestic fowl along the roads and in the fields, as the farmers would be apt to protest against such action with more vigor than might be pleasant for him.

Passing through a cornfield behind the house, the adventurous five climbed over the zigzag rail-fence which bounded Mr. Krowps' property, and soon found themselves in the woods upon the other side, Dick and Joel leading, Bob and Harry following closely, and Uncle Dan valiantly trudging on in the rear.

As they had now entered the woods and were in a neighborhood where they might expect to see game at any moment, Joel cautioned them to be wary, step lightly, say nothing, make as little noise as possible, and be ready to shoot at a moment's notice, a piece of advice to which, I am sorry to say, Uncle Dan and Bob paid but little attention.

That Uncle Dan should disregard it is not strange, since it would have given him the greatest pain to have been obliged to take the life of any living thing; but that Bob should have acted in a manner calculated to drive the game entirely out of reach may occasion surprise, until it is explained that at every step, that positive little gentleman was more and more deeply convinced that his vainglorious boasting of the morning had been, to say the least, very indiscreet; for Mr. Sturdy began to feel very much afraid that if he should see anything to fire at his self-established reputation as a marksman would be immediately destroyed.

Harry, who was the most nervous of them all, walked on tip-toe with an elaborate display of caution, peered hither and thither, now right, now left; now up, now down; now forward, now backward — ran to where Dick and Joel were quietly walking on with the soft step and watchful eye of practised huntsmen, and again ran back and joined Uncle Dan and Bob, who were following at some distance behind and talking in a loud tone of voice — and conducted himself altogether in such a nervous and excited manner that Joel at length could endure it no longer, and requested him curtly to "hold his horses;" a request which is not, however, to be taken in its literal sense, but was simply intended to convey Joel's desire for silence on the part of Mr. Cribbler.

A moment later Dick and Joel suddenly stopped — Joel's rifle was raised, there was a flash and a report, and down came a plump squirrel from the upper branches of a tall walnut-tree, shot through the head. Picking up the dead animal,

Joel placed it in Harry's game-bag and passed on without comment.

Uncle Dan, Bob and Harry looked at Joel with undisguised admiration, notwithstanding that Uncle Dan looked ruefully at the game-bag and said, "Poor thing! Poor thing! What a horrible invention gunpowder is, to be sure!" while Harry grew more nervous than ever, and Bob felt exceedingly uncomfortable as the thought that Joel might ask him to shoot at something disturbed his mind.

A moment later Dick's gun was raised and brought down another fine squirrel; soon afterward Joel and Dick fired simultaneously, and the result was a wild turkey and a rabbit.

The hunt became exciting, although a pang entered Uncle Dan's heart at each shot as if the bullet had penetrated it, and in the space of a few hours the game-bags were well filled.

At last, Dick and Joel stopped, and the latter, turning, beckoned to the three followers to draw nearer, at the same time signalling them to make as little noise as possible. Uncle Dan, Bob and Harry hurried forward and breathlessly inquired, "What is it?"

"Hush!" Joel whispered, "splendid shot!"

"Dear me!" exclaimed Uncle Dan, very loud.

"Whe — where is it?" inquired Bob, in an

equally loud tone of voice, at the same time stepping on a few dry twigs which broke with a sharp crackling sound.

"Hush!" whispered Joel — "you'll frighten him away, sure. There he is, up in that hickory-tree."

Glancing in the direction indicated by Joel they beheld seated on the lowest branch of a small hickory-tree, at not more than twenty yards distance, a large gray squirrel eating a nut which he held between his paws, while he eyed the newcomers with a saucy look, and did not seem to be at all disturbed by their unexpected presence.

"There he is," said Joel, passing his gun to Bob, "fire away!"

Bob began to turn pale. He mentally denounced his stupidity in boasting of his proficiency as a marksman when he actually knew no more about fire-arms than what he had learnt in patriotic but aimless efforts on the Fourth of July.

He raised the gun — he lowered it again — raised it a second time — "Hurry up," said Joel, impatiently, "he'll be gone in a minute."

Then Bob lowered the weapon again, looked appealingly at Uncle Dan, and said, "Uncle Dan, you haven't fired yet. Won't you try a shot?"

"Oh, dear, no!" said Uncle Dan, "I couldn't think of it."

"Don't wait," urged Joel, "it's not much of a shot — it's too easy — but I expected you'd look out for yourself. I want to see what kind of a hunter you are. Where will you put the ball, in the eye — or the ear — or the heart? Fire away."

"What dreadful particularity!" thought Uncle Dan.

Not much of a shot! Too easy! Wanted to see what kind of a hunter he was! It was enough to make Bob's knees tremble, and his heart sink within him. Nevertheless, seeing that there was no help for it, he raised the gun for the third time, took as good aim as his knowledge and the state of his nerves would permit, and pulled the trigger.

"Je — mi — ny Crickets!" exclaimed Joel, his two eyes as round as saucers and his face expressing the most unbounded astonishment, "that *was* a shot!"

It "*was* a shot" sure enough. For the gun, with a laudable determination to do all the execution in its power, recoiled with such sudden force that the valiant Mr. Sturdy went over backwards into a hazel-bush, while the smoke was still issuing from the muzzle of the weapon.

"Dear me! Dear me! Bob, my boy, are you hurt?" cried Uncle Dan, hastening to the assistance of his young friend.

MR. STURDY DOES NOT HIT THE GAME. — Page 198.

Bob scrambled to his feet and looked wildly about him.

"Did I hit him? Did I hit him?" he cried, running to the spot where the squirrel might have fallen and poking the grass with the barrel of the gun.

"Hit 'im?" shouted Joel, in a tone of immeasurable contempt, "No, you didn't even hit the tree. The squirrel's just as safe as ever he was, and a good deal safer, because he's out of our reach. What a shot!"

Bob's spirits immediately fell below zero; for from Joel's contemptuous tone he was convinced that his reputation as a marksman was forever lost in that neighborhood. With a comically sober face he again took charge of his game-bag, and, refusing to load and try again as Dick requested (for he knew that every succeeding display would but add to his discomfiture), took his place in line and went on without another word.

Whether the hunters had by this time killed all the game in the immediate neighborhood, or whether the noise of their firing had frightened the rest of them away, we are unable to say, but it must have been owing to either one or the other of these circumstances that they trudged on for fully half an hour after the last episode without finding anything that looked like "game." It is true that little birds were constantly seen resting upon the branches or flying from tree to tree, and that Joel had levelled his gun at them once or twice in order to display his skill, and as he remarked, "to keep his hand in."

But Uncle Dan had peremptorily forbidden all such cruel and unnecessary sport. And the little songsters flew about unmolested, twittering and singing to their heart's content.

In this manner they had rambled on for some time, and Dick had already proposed retracing their steps, as they had quite sufficient game to supply the table for several days to come, when they were suddenly startled by a shrill and prolonged " Hush !-h-h-h-h-h ! "

They turned quickly and beheld Harry gazing intently upward and gesticulating wildly with one hand. He was several yards behind them, and they hurried back to see the cause of his excitement.

"Hush-h-h! Give me a gun. I see it!"

"What is it?" asked his friends in a breath.

" A wild pigeon !"

"Where? Where?"

" Up there, in that tree !"

"I don't see it," said Joel.

"Neither do I," said Bob and Uncle Dan.

"Nor, I," said Dick.

"Well, I do," said Harry, excitedly, "give me your gun, quick!"

The gun was given, Harry raised it boldly, although it shook in his nervous hands, and fired.

Everybody looked to see the pigeon fall, and Bob even took several steps forward in order to catch it. But no such bird — nor any other — could be seen, either descending or ascending.

"You haven't hit it," said Bob.

"No, and he won't hit it," commented Joel.

"Why not?" inquired Harry, indignantly.

"Because it isn't there."

"Yes, it is," rejoined Harry, sharply, "I see it now. It's up there. Load the gun again, quick, and let me try again."

"Where is it, then?" asked the incredulous Joel, "I don't see it."

"Man alive," Harry burst out, "where are your eyes? There it is on that big crooked branch near the fork to the right."

"I see it," said Bob.

"So do I," said Uncle Dan.

"So do I," said Joel, with a grin, "but 't ain't no pigeon."

"What is it, then?" said Harry.

"It's an old bird's nest," said Joel, the grin perceptibly widening, "and it's been up there for three years."

The laugh which followed at Harry's expense was long, loud and hearty — none more so than Mr. Sturdy's, who was rejoiced to find that he was not the only one who had demonstrated his unskilfulness.

"Come on, Uncle Dan," said Dick, when the chorus of laughter had somewhat subsided — "I want to find you a shot before you go home. I know you can do better than Bob and Harry did."

"Oh, yes," thought Uncle Dan, chuckling to himself, "I can do better. If the poor creatures have no one else to fire at them they will be safe enough."

"There!" said Dick, after a few minutes of careful watching, "there's a rabbit. Quick. He's running away!"

Thus urged, Uncle Dan brought the gun to his shoulder, aimed, as he supposed, about five feet too high, and pulled the trigger.

In the next moment the gun was on the ground and Uncle Dan was rubbing his shoulder with all his might, while Joel and Dick greeted him with such ejaculations as "Bravo!" "Good!" "Well done!" "That's business!" and the like.

"Dear me!" exclaimed Uncle Dan, "how that gun does kick!"

"Never mind," said Dick, "you brought him down at any rate."

"I — what!"

"Hit — right through the head," said Joel.

Alas! it was only too true; for at this moment Harry approached with the dead rabbit and confirmed Joel's words.

The tears started into Uncle Dan's eyes. He took the rabbit from Harry, looked pityingly upon it, stroked its soft fur, and burst into a broken tone of mingled misery and self-reproach.

"Poor thing! Poor thing! Oh, how cruel — how cruel! My boys, I have been guilty of an action — a mean, wicked, cruel action — for which I can never forgive myself in the world. Here, Harry, take it. I can't bear it — I can't bear it!" and motioning to Joel to lead the way homeward, Uncle Dan followed in a state of gloomy depression, sorrow, and remorse, which sobered his buoyant-hearted companions and from which he did not recover for many days.

And thus unhappily ended Mr. Poldertot's first efforts at enjoyment in the country.

CHAPTER XIX.

An invitation to attend a festival. — And how Uncle Dan was compelled to go.

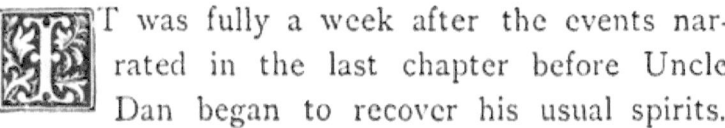T was fully a week after the events narrated in the last chapter before Uncle Dan began to recover his usual spirits. During this time he had steadily refused to accompany his young friends upon any of their numerous fishing, hunting, nutting, and exploring expeditions, with which the pleasant autumn days were passed, and busied himself instead with the safer, and to him equally interesting, pastimes of hunting for eggs in the barn, watching the harvest-work, driving home the cows, and taking long refreshing rambles along the winding country roads

But this could not always last. Bob, Dick and Harry were anxious that Uncle Dan should join them in the more exciting pleasures with which their time was occupied. At length a council of war was held, when it was unanimously decided that the very next time they ventured out together they would take Uncle Dan with them, "peaceably if they could, forcibly if they must."

An opportunity for carrying out this intention was not long delayed. For Joel came home from a trip to a neighboring village to say that he had met "Jim Maguire on the road, an' he'd given him an invite to a festival," which was to take place that very night, at Elm-Tree Hall, "and family and friends included."

"Oh, isn't that nice?" exclaimed Miss Caroline, to whom, it could not be said that the presence of the visitors had, up to this time been an unalloyed pleasure, since her usual household duties had by their advent been sensibly increased, "I hope we'll go."

"Goody! goody! goody!" cried Miss Mary, excitedly clapping her hands, "I'll go."

"Then I'm going, too," said little Hank, whose chief aim in this life was to secure as many privileges and enjoyments as his sister Mary.

"Dear me! A festival!" exclaimed Uncle Dan, adjusting his spectacles preparatory to reading a paper which Joel had brought from the village post-office, "A very good idea, my friends; excellent. I hope you will all go."

"Yes, we will, of course, we will," said little Bob, "and you're going to."

"I!" said Uncle Dan.

"Yes, you," said positive little Bob. "We've had enough of your moping about the house, sir, and we're going to put a stop to it. So make up your mind to come right along."

"Moping!" repeated Uncle Dan, "moping! How have I been moping, Bob?"

"Why," retorted Bob, boldly, — "haven't you buried yourself in the house, or crept along the roads like a snail, or hid yourself in the barn, while the rest of us have been having a glorious time in the woods? Why, we've been all over the country by this time, and you don't know anything about it. We're not going to submit to it any longer. You must go with us to-night." And as Bob said this with an air of the greatest determination and swept his forefinger down to emphasize his words, Uncle Dan looked helplessly around the room.

"Oh, yes, you must go," said Harry, as Uncle Dan's glance rested upon him.

"Certainly," said Miss Caroline, who was next mutely appealed to, "we can't do without you."

"Fact," was Dick's laconic comment.

"An ef you want to get thur sometime t'-night you'd better be a slickin' up, 'cause Elm-Tree Hall's a putty good stretch o' walkin' from h'yur an' so thur ain't no time to lose. Go 'long, Dan'l, it'll do you good," added Mr. Krowps, Sr.

Thus urged, Uncle Dan reluctantly retired to his room and soon reappeared clothed in his best attire, a suit of shining broadcloth, a necktie of immense proportions, the ends of which hung loosely over his immaculate white shirt-front, and the stiff silk-hat, which was by this time in a very doubtful state of gentility, since it looked as if it might recently have passed through the hands of a rag and bottle man. It had come into such frequent and violent contact with rafters in the barn, and the branches of trees, had tumbled once into the dust of the road and rolled along before a stiff breeze over a freshly cut corn-field, and had even been investigated by a pig with an inquiring turn of mind, who had inserted his snout into it when Uncle Dan had innocently left it on the grass while he mounted a ladder to pick apples, that it had quite lost its stiff and shining appearance.

"Now, Daniel," said Aunt Prudence, looking keenly at her husband, which made that worthy gentleman feel a trifle uneasy, "I want you to behave yourself to-night."

"Dear me!" exclaimed Uncle Dan, "you don't suppose I am going to do otherwise, do you?"

"I don't suppose anything," retorted Aunt Prudence, sharply, "only, as I am going with you, I want you to conduct yourself in a manner becoming your years — not like a school-boy."

Uncle Dan promised to comport himself with becoming dignity. And soon thereafter a merry company issued from the front door and, filing through the gate, turned to the right and passed down the road.

CHAPTER XX.

The renowned individuals who greeted Uncle Dan. — And the impressions created by the gallant Mr. Sturdy and the polite Mr. Cribbler.

AT the expiration of three-quarters of an hour they reached a long, low, wooden building — brilliantly illuminated with the light of half-a-dozen coal-oil lamps — from which the enlivening strains of a fiddle out of tune and a flute with a cold, proceeded to welcome all newcomers. Giving their hats and wraps to a cheerful little man at the door, who smiled profusely, nodded his head twice, and said, "Thank'ee — thank'ee," for every garment and article committed to his care — probably with a view to substantial recognition of his services later in the evening when these same articles should be returned to their respective owners, they entered the hall, where a number of couples were already promenading. The hall was still in an unfinished condition, for the walls were destitute of plaster, and the bare rafters, boards, and shingles of the roof were present to the eye of any one who would take the trouble to look at them. Against the walls on three sides of the room were rudely constructed booths, wherein were displayed a variety of home-made fancy articles, highly-colored chromos, flowers, fruits, and other objects calculated to captivate the rustic mind and deplete the rustic pocket.

As soon as Uncle Dan entered the room he was introduced to and welcomed by a gentleman whose height was not less than six feet, and whose rather angular and sun-reddened features would have betrayed him in any assemblage as a hard-working honest farmer, even though his body was enveloped in his present disguise, the costume of an Italian brigand.

"How air ye, sir — how air ye? I'm glad to see ye, sir. Hope ye'll feel to hum."

Uncle Dan responded heartily, mentally wondering why the gentleman had chosen to appear in such a ridiculously inappropriate costume. But the gentleman's next words enlightened him.

"We're a tryin' fur to hev a sort o' costoom festival, sir. It's fur the benefit o' the church down to Hog Holler. Ye see the young folks allowed as how sich an entertainment would drawr out the people kinder more plenty like than a plain sociable, an' so they've pet me inter them clothes. They ain't becomin' to me, I allow, but when a man makes a Napolyun Bunnyparte of himself he's got to dress accordin', — ain't thet so?"

Uncle Dan promptly assented, and cast a hasty glance around. Taking this as the evidence of a desire to become better acquainted, Napoleon generously offered his services as a medium of introduction between Uncle Dan and his friends.

And as Uncle Dan's particular acquaintances had already deserted him, he cheerfully accepted the offer and advanced with the emperor to greet "The Father of His Country," who was represented by a very little man with red hair, dressed in the costume of a modern cavalry officer.

Leaving Uncle Dan in the company of these great men, let us return to Bob, Dick and Harry, who had deserted Mr. Poldertot as the renowned Napoleon approached to welcome him.

"Who are those people, Joel?" inquired Dick, calling his companion's attention to an elderly gentleman and a neatly-dressed young lady who leaned on his arm, and who were slowly promenading just before them.

Joel, whose attention until this moment had been attracted by other matters, started as he saw them and uttered an involuntary exclamation of surprise.

"Why, that is Squire Brock and his daughter,"

said Joel. "I had no idea they would be here this evening."

"Ah!" said Dick.

"No," said Joel, "I had not."

"Why not?" asked Dick.

"Because, you see," said Joel, "Squire has just lost a daughter."

"Ah!" said Dick again — "sorry. How did it happen?"

"She ran away."

"She," repeated Dick, with that slow and easy deliberation which characterized this young gentleman's conversation, "ran — away."

"So — " drawled Dick, after a pause, appearing to regard with listless attention, one of the lamps at the other end of the room, but nevertheless keeping an observant eye upon the squire and his daughter, "— she — ran — away. Who with?"

"With no one," answered Joel. "Oh, he's a hard one, the Squire is; an' he treated her outrageous' bad." And Mr. Krowps shook his head and pursed his lips and glanced indignantly at the Squire.

"She was too good a girl to be bore down on the way he did. Bullying her an' ordering her around an' getting her ready to be married when she didn't want to be — an' ——"

"Married!" interrupted Dick.

"Yes, married," continued Joel, with considerable warmth, "wanted her to marry a city chap for his money — an' when she wouldn't do it — just tore 'round an' gave her a piece of his mind, an' nearly broke her heart. Poor thing! I've got her picture here. Let me show you."

Joel took from his pocket a long pocket-book, and after a moment's search amongst a miscellaneous assortment of bills, cards, and other papers, produced the photograph.

Now, why Dick should suddenly elevate his eyebrows and open his eyes as wide as possible and push out his lips as if about to give vent to a long, low whistle, we will not venture to explain; but we will only say that Mr. Doolittle regarded the picture with the air of a man who has worked over a Chinese puzzle for several consecutive days and has suddenly stumbled upon the solution of it when he least expected it.

"Do you know her?" asked Joel.

Without answering this question, Dick put his hand on Joel's arm and quietly led him into a corner of the room.

Leaving the result of Dick's action to be explained in succeeding pages, it behooves us to return without further delay to those gallant heroes, whom we have already too long ignored, namely, the celebrated Mr. Cribbler and the redoubtable Mr. Sturdy.

They had promenaded at first in the company of John and his fair sisters. But John and Mary soon leaving them it became their chivalrous duty to escort the gentle Caroline.

And so well did they perform it, with that gallantry and tact for which these bosom friends had ever been remarkable, that Miss Caroline spent the fleeting moments in a rapture of delight.

Indeed, so delightfully did Bob and Harry act their chivalric parts, so attentive were they to their young hostess, so polite to all the ladies, so generous in that they lavishly spent money in every booth, and loaded themselves down with a great variety of articles for which they could never have any possible use, and of half of which they did not even know the names, and acted generally in such a captivating manner, that all the ladies fell desperately in love with them and envied Miss Caroline Krowps to her heart's content.

At the same time we must make the acknowledgment, although with extreme regret, that this flattering success was not without one unfortunate circumstance. For, whereas it cannot be denied that the young ladies did unanimously agree that such pleasant, nice, handsome, generous, agreeable gentlemen as Mr. Sturdy and Mr. Cribbler it had never before been their good fortune to meet, there soon appeared a marked coolness upon the part of the young men who had come from various parts of the country to create a sensation as "beaux," and who were thus temporarily displaced in the thoughts and affections of their lady-loves by two insignificant little "city chaps." And when a simple rumor, how or by whom it was started no one knew, became generally known, to the effect that Mr. Sturdy was a great artist and had in preparation a picture from which he expected to realize a fabulous sum, and that Harry was an author, and was engaged upon a work that would make him wealthy and famous, the ladies were quite captivated, and gathered around our heroes, asking a host of questions and utterly ignored the disgusted "beaux," who had spent days of anxious thought in devising certain astounding, rainbow-like costumes in which they had made their appearance.

Under these circumstances it is not astonishing that Bob and Harry's conversation was, that evening, mainly carried on with the ladies, and that the young gentlemen left to their own devices should have gathered together in groups and indignantly discussed the situation.

If Bob and Harry saw the impressions which they were creating, they at least pretended to take no notice of them, but continued to conduct themselves in that irresistible manner for which they were so justly celebrated.

Whatever may have been their thoughts upon the subject, however, it is certain that they were not left long in ignorance of the peculiar state of affairs ; and if we assume that they were quite unconscious of the antagonistic feelings which they had unwittingly aroused in the hearts of the assembled gentlemen in "costoom," then it cannot be denied that they were most suddenly and rudely awakened from this state of blissful ignorance.

Now, when a gentleman stops in a booth at a fair or festival wherein there are a number of charming young ladies, and enters into an animated conversation with them, he is not apt to pay much attention to any conversation in which other parties may happen to be engaged in the next booth. But when the conversation in the next booth becomes gradually louder and more distinct, and passes through the thin board partition without much diminution of sound, it may happen that the gentleman, however much he may be engrossed in the charming society of the ladies, cannot fail to hear at least some of the words that are not intended for his ears; and, furthermore, when these chance words, thus unavoidably overheard, prove that an earnest discussion is going on about the gentleman himself, it is beyond the power of human nature not to pay a rather close attention to the utterances of the unknown speaker. And this was precisely the case with Bob and Harry.

They had reached the last booth but one on the south side of the building, and were laughing and talking (ever and always in a gentlemanly way of course) with a number of fairies gathered around a little puddle of water, a few rocks covered with green paper to represent moss, and a feeble fountain — (operated from the cellar by the efficient aid of a cistern-pump and a colored man at the rate of twenty-five cents an hour), — though what the whole arrangement was intended to represent, — water, fountain, rocks, green paper, fairies and all — the chief fairy herself could not have told you, when suddenly the words, "Said he could hit the bull's-eye every time," followed by a loud laugh from several masculine throats, attracted his attention.

"Yes," pursued the speaker, as soon as the laugh

had subsided, "said he could hit the bull's-eye every time."

"An' he didn't even kill a squirrel," said another voice, in a tone of contempt.

"No," said the first speaker — "come nowhere nigh one. He fired only onct, though, 'n' then the gun keeled him over flat."

"Keeled him over! Ha-ha-ha-ha!"

"An' he didn't hit nothin?" inquired another voice.

"Hit! He didn't come anywhere nigh hittin' the tree — let alone the squirrel. Jim Hawley told Sam Thompson that Joel Krowps told Hal Whitsell that the squirrel just sat there an' winked at him."

A perfect cannonade of laughter followed this spicy information.

"Bob," said Harry, nudging his friend, "they're talking about you."

Bob said nothing. But as the brilliancy of his politeness and gallantry suddenly left him, and as he began to answer the fairies in monosyllables, it is safe to presume that the conversation had made an impression upon him.

"That ain't all," chimed in another voice, which had not previously been heard, "t' other feller done worse 'n that one did. T'other feller blazed away at an old bird's nest 'cause he thought 'twas game."

Another roar of laughter followed. Even the fairies began to titter. Miss Caroline looked helpless and embarrassed. Bob's choleric nature was fast working him into a passion, and Harry looked meekly around with a very red face and a sheepish expression.

"But we'll fix 'em to-night," said one of the speakers.

"You better believe!" observed another.

"But what's goin' to be done?" inquired a third.

A reply was made but in so low a tone that it was inaudible.

But Bob had heard enough. What! Should he hear his bosom friend and himself thus mysteriously threatened, and tamely submit? Would he thus be menaced with undeserved and unknown danger and make no effort to punish the audacious authors of it? Never! His mind was made up. He would not remain idle. He would act.

And with this noble determination animating him, Bob bade the fair ladies a stately adieu — said bravely, "This thing must be attended to and I'm going to attend to it!" and walked boldly out of the booth with his head erect and his hands clenched.

"Oh, Mr. Cribbler!" cried Miss Caroline Krowps, anxiously clasping her hands, "don't let Mr. Sturdy fight."

"Never fear," said Mr. Cribbler, reassuringly, "Bob knows better."

CHAPTER XXI.

Wherein is related how Mr. Robert Sturdy interrupted the peaceful conversation of the most distinguished people in the world; and invoked the protection of the law.

WHEN Uncle Dan was last mentioned in these pages he was in the act of making his acknowledgments to the "Father of His Country," who was represented by a small gentleman with red hair, dressed in a suit of modern cavalry clothes. Escorted by this historic personage, in company with the "Scourge of Europe," Uncle Dan passed through the room, and was introduced to a great number of celebrated people, all of whom welcomed him with the greatest cordiality, while some made the most interesting inquiries about the state of his health, and others earnestly begged him to make himself "to home."

Had Uncle Dan possessed the remotest inclination to criticise it is possible that he would have indulged in some justifiable reflections upon the manner, appearance, conversation, and costume of the renowned personages with whom it was his present good fortune to become acquainted. For, had he paid the slightest attention to these matters, it must have struck him as rather singular that Daniel Webster should have appeared in a suit of yellow jeans and a Mexican sombrero and have been so bashful that he blushed to the roots of his hair the moment a word was said to him. And when Cromwell came before Uncle Dan, dressed like a Franciscan monk, with the important information that "the crawps this year looks a moughty sight better 'n th' did las' year," and when Robin Hood, in the person of a lean gentleman with a sallow complexion, sauntered by with the "Maid of Orleans," a buxom lass who had every appearance of being fat, fair and forty, and who carried a baby with an evident air of proprietary right, it would not have been strange if Uncle Dan had glanced about him with some surprise, and felt that in a historical point of view things were slightly mixed.

But, "dear me!" as Uncle Dan would probably have remarked — if he had remarked anything at all — he thought nothing about it — nothing whatever. And so far was Uncle Dan's mind from a condition of finding fault with anything or anybody, that the humble historian is sincerely of the opinion, that if George Washington had appeared in the uniform of a British red-coat or a Hessian soldier it would not have impressed him as being in the slightest degree inappropriate or ridiculous.

On the contrary, Uncle Dan entered with the greatest zest and interest into the conversations which were carried on around him, so that in the course of the evening he knew more about country life and manners — corn, oats, wheat, and crops in general — horses, cows, and pigs — not to mention various standard ailments, such as "rheumatiz" "spepsy," "fever 'n' ager," and the like than he had ever known before in all his life.

Had no interruption occurred Uncle Dan might have continued to pass the time in this pleasant manner until the close of the festival and the departure of the people brought the conversations to a close, and caused his return homewards with his friends. But Uncle Dan was just in the midst of an animated political discussion with a group of gentlemen, composed of such world-renowned characters as General Lafayette, General Washington, Sir Walter Scott, Napoleon, Kit Carson, Montezuma, the Duke of Wellington, and Andrew Jackson, when he felt his arm touched by the end of a finger, while a voice, trembling with emotion, uttered the words, "Uncle Dan!"

"Why — dear me! — Bob!" exclaimed Uncle Dan, as he turned and beheld his diminutive friend standing before him with his hands clenched, his face flushed, and a general appearance of being in a state of violent agitation, "What is the matter?"

Bob shook his head till his bushy hair quivered, opened and closed his mouth and eyes two or three times in succession, and alarmed Uncle Dan by concluding these singular performances by a belligerent demonstration with his fists as if he were threatening the distinguished group before him and inviting them all in a pugilistic sense to "come on."

As Mr. Sturdy made no reply to his question, Uncle Dan was constrained to inquire again in a tone of deep concern, "Dear me! Dear me! Bob, my dear boy, what can be the matter? Has anything gone wrong?"

"Yes, sir," exclaimed Mr. Sturdy, tragically waving his hand above his head, "something *has* gone wrong!"

"Dear me!" said Uncle Dan, while the group of distinguished people gathered around Bob with anxious faces to hear the news; in their eagerness entirely forgetting their individuality, insomuch that Bonaparte might have been seen leaning in a friendly manner on the Duke of Wellington's shoulder, while Andrew Jackson and Sir Walter Scott stood arm in arm.

But Bob was not to be beguiled into a simple statement of his grievance. The occasion demanded more than this. The occasion demanded prompt and efficient action. And in the great mind of Mr. Sturdy a plan had already been adopted whereby the action should be both prompt and efficient. Wherefore Mr. Sturdy electrified his hearers by inquiring in a determined tone, "Is there any one here who is authorized to make an arrest?"

"Who?" "Where?" "What?" "What is it?" "Anybody hurt?" "Who did it?" "What's the matter?" were the exclamations that followed the unexpected question.

"I want to know," repeated Bob, giving his curly hair a vigorous shake and speaking in the same determined tone, "whether there is any one here who is authorized to make an arrest?"

"Waal," observed a wiry gentleman, whose scarred and weather-beaten face gave him the appearance of a veteran of forty winters, and who, in a pair of clay-colored trousers tucked into the tops of a pair of kip-leather boots, a red flannel shirt and a slouched hat, was known during the evening as "Garibaldi," "Waal, ef ye're sot onto it, young man, I s'pose I'll hev t' obleege ye, seein' as I'm the constabul fur this h'yur deestrick."

"Then, sir," said Bob, promptly, "please follow me. Uncle Dan, come on. And," as a prudent thought entered his mind, "if any of these gentlemen would like to go with us to see fair play, I will be very much obliged to them."

Then, Mr. Robert Sturdy pushed his fingers through his hair, gave his head a final shake, and strode impressively away; leaving Uncle Dan and the "constabul" and the rest of the company to follow at their pleasure. Which they accordingly did in a mingled state of surprise, bewilderment, and expectation.

CHAPTER XXII.

How Mr. Sturdy disappointed the law and the people. — His extraordinary and distressing adventure in the dark.

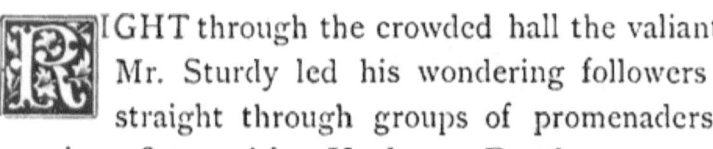IGHT through the crowded hall the valiant Mr. Sturdy led his wondering followers; straight through groups of promenaders, gypsies, flower-girls, Yankees, Dutch matrons, Irish lads, and heroes of every country, age, and description, all of whom were so deeply impressed with Mr. Sturdy's important bearing and determined air that they made way for him as soon as they saw him coming, stared at him in silent amazement as he passed, and then quietly fell in line and followed after under a dim conviction that something startling was about to transpire.

On went Mr. Sturdy — on, without looking to the right or to the left, or seemingly caring whether he was followed by one individual or ten thousand — on he went directly to the booth where the conspirators had been in session — on until within a few feet of it. Then Mr. Sturdy stopped, and waving his hand in rather a theatrical manner, exclaimed in a firm tone of voice, "Constable, arrest the parties in that booth!"

Without assuming any especial official dignity, but rather in a free and easy manner, with his hands in his pockets, the constable sauntered past Mr. Sturdy and approached the booth. They crowded around him, that eager train. A breathless silence fell upon them all. He broke in — he entered — he came out again — he said, "Thur ain't nobody thur!"

Then Bob ran forward — entered and came out again with a look of blank astonishment. Then Uncle Dan also entered, followed by as many of the distinguished individuals as could get into the booth with him. It was only too true. The booth was empty, and all Bob's trouble had been for naught. Poor Bob was crestfallen and subdued.

In as few words as possible our unfortunate hero related what had occurred.

"But, Bob, my boy," said Uncle Dan, "why did you not go into the booth as soon as you overheard the conversation and demand an explanation?"

"Oh — I — I — don't know," said Bob.

And when the assembled congress of nations found that no murder or assault had been committed, that no burglar had been caught, pickpocket arrested, or even a small boy detected in the act of surreptitiously gaining admittance through a back window, they sauntered away, mentally indignant with Mr. Sturdy for having plunged them into a state of excitement and expectation to no purpose, and from that moment used poor Mr. Sturdy as an object of ridicule and derision. Even the ladies turned against him and made fun of him. For he had lost his buoyant spirits, and was no more the captivating, polite, attentive gentleman who had won their hearts by his witty conversation, generous purchases and brilliant manners.

Bob could not help witnessing the covert glances or occasionally hearing the sly laughter and subdued remarks with which his appearance was greeted in every part of the room. So annoying did this at length become that he determined to go away, and mentally vowed that he would return to the city at the first opportunity.

Dick had already left the hall, Harry was nowhere to be seen, and Uncle Dan was so deeply engaged in an interesting conversation about the relation which this year's grasshoppers bore to next year's crops, that Bob determined not to disturb him. And so quietly receiving his hat from the little man at the door, and rewarding that supple individual with a silver dime, Bob stole forth into the open air with a heavy heart.

Thus, in a moment, do our pleasures turn to griefs.

With a profound sigh Bob turned his back upon the building, and, avoiding the more frequented road by which he had come, struck into a small wood-path, hoping by this means to reach Farmer Krowps' house without observation or molestation.

Had Bob cast a glance behind him as he left the road to follow the narrower path it is highly probable that he would have been somewhat startled by a singular occurrence which just at that moment took place; and that he would have proceeded along the path he had chosen with watchful suspicion — had he not hesitated to go that way altogether. But he saw nothing, and so he passed on in blissful ignorance that just as he turned away from the commonly-used road, six shadows, emerging from the cover of darkness, under the hall steps, slid noiselessly and in a stooping posture across the intervening space between the building and the trees, and disappeared hastily into the woods some distance to the right of the path over which Bob was dejectedly picking his way.

It was a charcoal-burner's path that Bob had chosen, and as he walked along he passed, every now and then, tent-shaped piles of wood in a process of combustion. But paying no attention to these sights, which under other circumstances would have enlisted his eager attention, he continued his journey with his head bowed upon his breast, mechanically hunting his way over the winding path and through the darkness, engrossed in thought.

At length his thoughts broke forth in words, and he soliloquized aloud, "Shoot! Huh! Shoot, indeed! Not my fault that I didn't hit the mark — loaded the old thing up to the muzzle — I know he did. Knock me down? Of course it did. 'Twould have knocked down an ox. Never mind. If any of 'em come to town I'll get even. They can't impose on us in that way. If there's a law in the land——" but here his soliloquy was unceremoniously cut short. For just then his foot struck an obstruction (afterward he remembered that it felt like a string stretched across the path), and, groping wildly with his hands extended, down he came full length upon the ground.

Bob arose as soon as possible, affectionately rubbing the end of his nose, which had received a rap that started the tears from his eyes. He did not hear the suppressed laughter behind the tree to his left, or catch the flash of a lantern which illuminated the path behind him for a moment, but, rubbing his bruised nose, Bob strode onward, grumbling and discontented.

Grumbling and discontented he had only taken a few steps when he was suddenly enveloped, overwhelmed, chilled, stunned and thoroughly drenched by a shower of cold spring water poured from the branches of a tree that overhung the road.

"You outra — rageous vil — villains! Br-r-r! Br-r-r! Whoever you are — Br-r-r! Vr-r-sh! Come down — You cow — cowards! Come down — I say — Br-r-r! And I'll thrash you — every one of you — Vr-r-rsh! — within an inch of your lives!" spluttered the wet and dripping Mr. Sturdy, shaking his clenched hand at the darkness above him.

Mr. Sturdy was enraged or he would never so far have forgotten himself as to threaten unknown persons in this rash and foolish way. But the gentlest-minded reader will agree that it is exceedingly provoking to be unexpectedly deluged on a cool night, on a lonely country path, and in one's best clothes, by an unlimited quantity of cold water.

"I dare you to come down!" cried Mr. Sturdy, shaking his fist aloft.

An ominous rattling followed, and then while his

face was upturned and his arms still extended, there came pattering down upon him a bucketful of hickory-nuts and walnuts. Down they came, blinding him, bruising him, — on his eyes, nose, lips, chin — everywhere; raising little red mounds all over his face, as marks of their violence.

"Villains! Knaves!" shouted the now maddened Mr. Sturdy, dancing up and down with pain and rage, "I'll shoot the first man, woman or child I see up there!" utterly forgetful of the fact that he had nothing in the shape of firearms in his possession.

A derisive chorus of laughter greeted this vain threat, followed by such ironical advice, as "Go and tell your mother she wants you." "Oh, fight a duel." "Shoot with the butt end of the gun, bubby." "Trot home, little boy, trot home."

Burning with rage, but feeling the uselessness of contending with his unseen foe, Bob plunged blindly forward.

Another deluge of water, another shower of nuts, and the bold Mr. Sturdy, losing all control of himself, ran, stumbled and staggered, shrieking epithets and shouting threats at the top of his voice until he reached the welcome shelter of Farmer Krowps' hospitable home, and fell panting and exhausted into Uncle Dan's arms.

CHAPTER XXIII.

Dick tells Uncle Dan a strange piece of news. — The girl. — "She must be found."

NO words can express the astonishment, the grief, the indignation which Uncle Dan felt when Bob had fully narrated all the particulars of the shabby trick that had been played upon him.

Regarding himself as in a certain sense responsible for the safety and well-being of his youthful friends, the distressed Mr. Poldertot reproached himself beyond measure for having permitted Bob to escape from his watchful care. True, as soon as Uncle Dan had learnt of Bob's departure from the hall, he had bidden a hasty adieu to General Washington, General Lafayette, Sir Walter Scott, and the whole galaxy of illustrious individuals who had clustered around him, and, finding Mr. Krowps ready to accompany him, made all haste homeward in the hope of overtaking Bob, or Dick and Harry, all of whom had left the scene of the festivities without as much as saying, "Good night," to their anxious friend and protector.

Harry was overtaken gallantly escorting the young ladies homeward. But that gentleman knew nothing of either of his boon companions. And so Uncle Dan pushed on again with increased anxiety and speed to the great amusement of Farmer Krowps, who could not understand why Dan'l should be so foolishly solicitous about a pa'cel o' young men, who were evidently well able to take care of themselves.

Consequently Uncle Dan had reached the house a few moments before Bob entered it.

"My dear boy," said Uncle Dan, with a look of the deepest sympathy on his ruddy countenance, while he busily rubbed Bob's battered face with a flannel rag saturated with arnica, "It is too bad — it really is too bad. I don't see how any one could have been capable of so mean an action."

"You ought to have gone home with him. The idea of letting him go alone through the woods at this time of night! But they're all alike. If one of you gets killed some day, don't say I didn't warn you."

It was Aunt Prudence who said these words, and it was Aunt Prudence who, having said them in a sharp, reproving tone, fell vigorously to work upon a pair of woollen socks which she was knitting for Uncle Dan.

"I know, Prudence, I know," said Uncle Dan, sorrowfully, while he made poor Bob wince with the vigor of his benevolent ministrations, "no one regrets the circumstance more than I do. I can never forgive myself — never. I wish I had kept them near me all the evening. This thing shall never happen again if I can prevent it."

"Huh!" retorted Aunt Prudence, "lock the stable door after the horse is stolen, as usual."

"Come, come, Prue," said Sister Sarah, "don't be hard on him."

"I'm not hard on him," replied Aunt Prudence, snapping her needles back and forth with great energy; "I'm only telling the truth. And if he keeps on rubbing that boy and lets him sit there in his wet clothes he'll catch his death of cold and wet, and then Daniel will say it's my fault, because I didn't tell him."

"Dear me! dear me!" said Uncle Dan, with the deepest contrition manifested in the tone of his voice and the expression of his face, "how exceedingly stupid I am! He's wet through. My dear boy, go right to your room and change your clothes and go to bed. Harry, go up and help him. Sister Sarah, would it be asking too much to ask you to make a warm cup of tea? If Bob should get sick I don't know what I would do."

"No, I suppose not," said Aunt Prudence, with severe irony.

Nevertheless, the good lady laid aside her knitting, and actively assisted Sister Sarah in preparing the desired cup of tea, while Harry and Uncle Dan led the bruised and crestfallen Mr. Sturdy to his room and put him to bed; an operation that was not accomplished to the satisfaction of Uncle Dan until Bob was almost smothered beneath a pile of blankets and quilts that would have started the perspiration out of an Arctic explorer in Greenland.

When everything had been done for Bob that Uncle Dan's tender solicitude and sympathy could devise, the latter, leaving Harry in the room, returned to the lower story and found that John and Joel had returned, but without Dick.

"Dear me! dear me!" groaned Uncle Dan, as with Bob's recent experience in his mind, the most exquisite fears concerning Dick's safety began to torture him, "come home without Dick? Well — well! And don't you know where he is now?"

"Now, I'm not going to have you tramping through the woods at this time of the night," spoke up Aunt Prudence with remarkable promptness, "you stay home."

"Dear me, Prudence, how sharp you are! And you don't know where Dick is, John?"

"No, sir," said John.

"Nor you, Joel?"

Joel answered in the negative, and then asked for Bob and Harry. The complete and evidently genuine astonishment of the brothers upon being informed of the experience through which Bob had that evening passed was enough to destroy any latent suspicion that may have lurked in the minds of any one present, that they had in any way participated in the attack, or even knew that it had been designed.

"Whew-w-w!" exclaimed Joel.

"That beats anything I ever heard," said his brother.

"D'you know who done it?" asked Farmer Krowps.

"No," said Joel, promptly, "I left 'fore Bob, an' everything was lovely then."

"Don't know nothing about it," said John.

Joel, upon being further pressed in reference to Dick, remembered that the missing young man had shown considerable attention to Miss Brock.

"Miss Brock?" said Uncle Dan. "Then perhaps he accompanied her home."

"Perhaps so," said Joel.

"Then," said Uncle Dan, rising, "I will know where to find him."

"Daniel," said Aunt Prudence, turning her keen eyes upon her worthy spouse, "what are you going to do?"

"I am going to meet Dick."

"You are going to do nothing of the kind, Daniel."

"Yes, I am, Prudence."

"You are not, Daniel."

"I tell you, Prudence, I am."

It was a novel sight to see Uncle Dan daring to oppose his sharp and determined wife. But all his fears were aroused, and nothing could swerve him from his noble determination to find Dick.

"Dan'l — say, Dan'l," said Farmer Krowps, "let that young man alone. He'll take care o' himself better'n you kin."

"Nobody knows the danger he may be in at this moment," said anxious Uncle Dan.

"He's all right," said Joel.

"Of course he is," seconded his brother.

"Don't go out, Uncle Dan," plead Miss Mary, "something might happen to you."

"Oh, you had better stay," added her mother, "you'd be sure to get lost in the woods."

"If you're trying to convince him," said Aunt Prudence, while her eyes and her knitting-needles snapped simultaneously, "you're trying a very useless thing. You might as well talk to the side of the house. But I say he shan't go, and that's the end of it."

"Prudence," said Uncle Dan, mildly, but firmly, "you know that I have the greatest respect for your wishes, and under ordinary circumstances I always comply with them. But in this instance I feel that duty calls me —— "

"Fiddlesticks!" interrupted Aunt Prudence.

"And consequently I must go," concluded Uncle Dan.

It can never be known what would have been the result of this great controversy had it continued longer. But it was destined to be suddenly cut short by the arrival of the very young gentleman who was the occasion of it, and who thus unexpectedly decided it in favor of Aunt Prudence.

"And now," said Farmer Krowps, after Dick had been questioned and made fun of and had been told of Bob's adventure, and had quietly borne and listened to it all, in his imperturbable manner, "it's time all honest folks was in bed an' rogues on the road thur. Airly to bed, airly to rise, makes a man healthy, an' wealthy, an' wise. Ain't that so, Dan'l. Mother, will you read the chapter? Heft down the book thur, Jole, an' slide it 'long to mother."

Sister Sarah having read the customary chapter, and Uncle Dan having offered a short prayer, the members of this pleasant company dispersed to their rooms.

"Uncle Dan," said Dick, as Mr. Poldertot arose to leave the room, "I want to speak to you a moment."

"Certainly, certainly," said Uncle Dan, wondering what confidence his usually reticent young friend had to impart, while he led the way to the parlor.

"Uncle Dan," said Dick, coming to the point with unusual directness and brevity, "I am going to town to-morrow"

"Going to town, Dick? Dear me! Why not wait until we all go?"

"Because," said Dick, "I can't."

"Because," repeated Uncle Dan, "you can't. Why?"

"There is a matter of business that needs my immediate attention."

"Have you heard from town, Dick?"

"No, sir."

"Did you know about this before?"

"Not until within the last hour or two."

"Dear me! Dear me!"

"And I want to tell you about it. The business is, to some parties, a matter of great importance. Has Joel told you about Squire Brock's daughter?"

"Yes — yes. How sad — how sad!"

"And you remember the young lady left her home to avoid marrying a man who was repulsive to her?"

"Perfectly, Dick. A noble girl, my boy, a noble girl."

"Well," said Dick, "that young lady may safely return. Her father bitterly repents his course, and is doing everything possible to find her. The other daughter, with whom I became acquainted this evening, told me that she fears the absence of her sister will seriously affect her father's health, both in mind and body, unless her whereabouts are discovered. They have advertised and sought for her in vain. The young lady attended the festival much against her own inclinations and only because her father desired it, as he hoped that she might be able to hear something about her sister there."

"Dear me!" said Uncle Dan, with emotion, "Dear me!"

"I learned from the young lady that her sister is supposed to be still in the city. She was last seen there in a hotel where she had been stopping. She disappeared upon being recognized by a friend who happened to stop there one day, and no one has been able to find her since. But it is believed that she is still in or near the city, as she was poorly provided with means and could not travel very far."

"Poor child!" exclaimed Uncle Dan, sorrowfully shaking his head, "a stranger, hiding from her friends, alone, unprotected, poor! Dear me! What must become of her!"

"Consequently she must be found."

"She must, Dick, she must."

"And as soon as possible."

"As soon as possible, Dick — without a moment's delay. But how can she be found, Dick? Who will find her?"

Uncle Dan looked almost as much concerned as if the young lady was his own daughter.

"I intend to try," said Dick.

"You, Dick!" Uncle Dan regarded his young friend with evident admiration and approval. "So you have enlisted in the cause of the ladies, have you, you sly rogue?" said Uncle Dan, while there was a peculiar mellowness in the tone of his pleasant, hearty voice, "Well, well, Dick, success go with you."

"You have not inquired," said Dick, "who the gentleman is who has caused all this trouble."

"True. But I don't know him, Dick, do I?"

Dick nodded his head.

"Dear me! Who can it be?"

"He is," said Dick, suddenly roused into an excitement that was quite unusual with him, and striking the table with his clenched hand, "one of the meanest villains out of jail."

"Dear me!" exclaimed Uncle Dan; and in his astonishment he wiped his face with a chair-tidy.

"The worst scoundrel between here and San Francisco."

"Well — well — Dick! Tell me his name."

"Rolf Seppeld."

"Rolf Seppeld!" cried Uncle Dan, "impossible!"

"That is what I thought," said Dick, nervously rubbing the sides of his chair, "until I saw him."

"Saw him! Dear me! Where?"

"In the village — at the festival — in disguise.

But I recognized him. Miss Brock tells me that he haunted her sister — with her father's approval — until she could bear it no longer. Oh — he'll have to pay for it!"

"But," continued Uncle Dan, "I thought his affections were placed in quite a different quarter. I thought he was in love with Miss Bulbous."

"So I thought," said Dick, "but the rascal is playing double. I'll unmask him though — so quick it will make his head swim."

"And that reminds me — " Uncle Dan was suddenly stricken with remorse, "that I promised to speak a good word to the professor in Bob's behalf and I forgot all about it. I must attend to it at once as soon as we go home."

"Well," said Dick, his naturally indolent manner returning, "I suppose it's about time to go to bed."

"So it is," said Uncle Dan, rising. Then suddenly laying his two broad hands upon his young friend's shoulders, Uncle Dan looked gratefully into his face, and, while his eyes sparkled with a suspicious moisture, said, "Dick, my good fellow, I can't tell you how much I thank you for interesting yourself in the cause of this oppressed girl. Whatever may be the result, my boy, you will have a precious and a sure reward. I am convinced from what I have heard that Mr. Seppeld is a dangerous man. And if I can do anything to aid you, Dick, you can count upon my heartiest assistance."

"I am sure of that," said Dick.

"And Bob and Harry, whatever may be the work you have to do, will only be too glad to help you all they can."

"I know that, too," said Dick.

"I presume you start in the morning?"

"Yes, sir; at about five o'clock."

"So early?"

"I want to catch the first train. I have an idea — and — well, I want to get away without the necessity of leave-taking."

"But that will seem rude."

"Oh," said Dick, yawning, "I hate good-byes."

"But what can I say?"

"Say that important business called me home."

"Yes, but Aunt Prudence — she'll worry it out of me."

"Tell her the particulars — but don't tell any one else."

"Very well; and now Dick, good night. And, lest you should be on your way before I get up — for you know I'm a heavy sleeper, my boy — Good-bye."

"Good-bye," said Dick, and Uncle Dan smilingly withdrew.

But a half hour after Dick was sitting in the same chair intently regarding a photograph which he held in his hand.

And in the morning he was gone.

CHAPTER XXIV.

Mr. Cliphart is herewith presented, and announces an approaching serenade.

BOB and Harry had often assured each other that as soon as their self-imposed vacation was over they would go diligently to work on the great picture of Napoleon and the Great American Novel, and never leave those stupendous works of art until they were completed. But genius is erratic and will not always cater to the inclinations or submit to the will of its possessor. Wherefore it is quite true, albeit we are loth to record it, that the brush and the pen were still idle upon the third day of the return of our heroes to the city. And, upon the very afternoon of that same day, Mr. Cribbler and Mr. Sturdy might have been seen sauntering along the streets of the city as slowly and as unconcernedly as if the millions of their countrymen were not awaiting in breathless anxiety and suspense the happy announcement that the two immortal productions were ready for the public gaze.

They were thus leisurely proceeding, careless of the day and thoughtless of the morrow, when their peaceful meditations were rudely disturbed by a heavy slap upon Bob's shoulder.

The friends turned hastily around, Bob prepared to annihilate the aggressor with the lightning of his eye and his ever-ready forefinger, when they saw Mr. Doolittle smiling down upon them, in company with a very tall, broad, light-haired, and awkward-looking gentleman, who was attired in a coarse, gray woollen shirt, a pair of brown trousers, patched at the knees, and a slouched hat.

"Mr. Sturdy," said Dick, with an unusual assumption of politeness, "Mr. Cliphart. Mr. Cribbler — Mr. Cliphart."

Mr. Cliphart nodded, but kept his body straight. Wherefore it may be presumed that Mr. Cliphart felt the danger of trusting that body out of his control in an attempt to bow. But Mr. Cliphart's voice — a deep and somewhat husky one — hastened to make amends for the short-comings of Mr. Cliphart's body, by saying, —

"Goot so — goot so; an' how is dengs?"

"Excellent," said Bob; "couldn't be better."

"Goot so. But I dell you wat, yentlemans, times is hart."

The "yentlemans" having silently acquiesced by

gravely inclining their heads, Mr. Cliphart considerately dropped a grain of comfort, by adding, —

"But we will see better times — sure. If not to-day, den to-morrow; if not to-morrow, den de nex' day; if not de nex' day, den some udder times. Eh, wat?"

"Certainly," said Dick.

"Of course," added Harry.

"Not a doubt of it," said Bob.

"But I dell you wat, yentlemans, if de times is bat, it makes notting: we will haf en liddle bit fun an' plaseer anyhow — is it not so?"

The trio nodded their heads.

"So I say to my friendt — dat is en old friendt mit namens Brankey — I say to him, 'Let uns haf en liddle mooseek.' An' he say, 'All ride.' An' I say, 'Let uns do en liddle saranaden.' An' he say, 'All ride.' Naw, who you denk we will saranaden, yentlemans?"

The yentlemans were unable to say.

"I knowed it," said Mr. Cliphart, joyfully, "we will saranaden de professor's dochter."

"The professor's daughter!" said Dick. "What is her name?"

"Naw, dat is easy to say. Her namens, dat is Boollabus. You know Bella Boollabus?"

Had they been told that Mr. Cliphart intended

to marry the young lady, they could hardly have been more surprised.

"Naw," went on Mr. Cliphart, with awkward gesticulation, "why not? Bella is en goot girl."

"Oh, undoubtedly," said Dick.

"So I denk. Derefore we will gif her some mooseek to-night. An' if you will comen, yentlemans, you will hearen' some nice mooseek."

Thanking him for his invitation, the three friends assured Mr. Cliphart that it would afford them the greatest pleasure to listen to the serenade, and then bidding him a pleasant "good day," they left him, determined to be present before the professor's house that evening and learn what kind of music it was with which the chivalrous Mr. Cliphart expected to favor the gentle Bella Bulbous.

"Bob," said Dick, "that's rival No. 2. Have you seen rival No. 1 lately?"

"I haven't any rivals," said Bob. "Bella Bulbous is as true as steel."

"Just so," said Dick, drily, "they all are. But have you seen Rolf Seppeld lately?"

"No; have you?"

"Yes," said Dick, "and he has written a long letter to the professor."

"You don't say!" cried Bob, anxiously. "Do you know what it is about?"

"The substance of it is that he demands the hand of Bella Bulbous."

"Demands!"

"Yes."

"Who told you so?"

"Bella."

"On what grounds does he demand?"

"She did not know. There is a secret between the professor and Seppeld. Seppeld has some claim on the professor, and he is using it to win the professor's daughter. And with vigor, too, for the professor threatens to disinherit her and drive her out of the house unless she accepts Rolf. In fact, he acts like a second edition of Squire Brock."

"Dick," said Bob, raising his forefinger above his head, "Bella Bulbous will never marry Rolf Seppeld."

"Check!" said Dick.

"Sooner than see her subjected to annoyance from him or any other man," and the forefinger came down with the sweep of a sword, "I'd marry her to-morrow."

"Checkmate!" cried Dick.

And then they parted.

But it might have been observed that Mr. Doolittle was more than usually thoughtful as he slowly passed along; and that Bob and Harry, as they disappeared in the opposite direction, were very grave and quiet.

They were touched by the shadow of a coming change, when the hitherto indissoluble trio, Bob, Dick, and Harry, should, if not entirely destroyed, lose a part, at least, of its old-time happiness and glory; when the ties that bound them now in an unshaken bond of confidence and friendship should be superseded, though not weakened, by the new and binding ties of marriage.

For it cannot be denied that marriage changes many things; and that many a friendship hitherto unbroken, many a gay companionship that youthful hearts in happy days have formed, will lose their freshness and their power, if they do not altogether fade away, before the new and all-important relations that are cemented at the altar.

CHAPTER XXV.

A mysterious shadow; and a silent watcher.

A BEAUTIFUL, clear summer night, illuminated by the full moon whose bright and mellow light is only disturbed now and then by a fleeting cloud. The silvery light falls softly and purely upon the silent, sleeping city, and chases away the trooping shadows from many a nook and corner where shadows love to lie. Broadly do these beams rest upon the roofs of houses and upon the almost deserted streets; and as they touch one street with their peculiar bright and mellow radiance they flood the front of a two-story brick row, which looks as if its tenants had departed long ago and abandoned it to silence and decay. For, with its closed doors and blinds, it looks in the ghostly moonlight like a spectre building of the past. Which it is not, however, for from the centre of the building projects a rusty iron rod upon which there hangs suspended an old, time-worn, weather-beaten sign, which, though it squeaks and creaks dismally in every passing breeze, and thus heightens the weird and ghostly effect of the time and place, nevertheless bears upon its surface, in letters quaint and olden, the legend which betrays the profession and occupation of that renowned musician, the worthy Professor Bulbous.

There are apparently no signs of life in this silent moonlit neighborhood. And yet, if one will look carefully at a point behind one end of the row of buildings one may see, crouched down close to the ground and partially hidden by a cheap board fence, a dark figure. From the manner in which this figure occasionally rises, and, peering forth with the greatest caution, eagerly scans the street and then crouches down again in hiding, it may be rightfully supposed that it is thus mysteriously watching for and awaiting the arrival of some person or event. But whether for a good purpose or a bad one, time and future narrative alone can tell.

A broad, black shadow lies upon the centre of the pavement directly before the professor's house, and tapers into a slender line which leads to the end of the row and is there lost in the shadow of the lower board of the fence adjoining. The shadow does not move as the moon creeps along the heavens, but lies, always, dark and sombre, in the same place. The shadows of the trees that line the street, the shadows of the slender glass-topped lamp-posts, the shadow of the wooden stairs before the house, even the shadow of the mournful old tin sign move as the moon moves, and seem to play hide-and-seek with that refulgent planet. All other shadows move in order as eminently proper shadows always do. But this one dark shadow, with its mysterious tail, lies upon the moonlit walk like a blot upon the fair page of a book, like a crime upon the record of a life — immovable, unchangeable, solemn, sombre, still.

What can it be? And the silent watcher, crouching there in the shelter of the house and fence, who is he? And what is he waiting for so quietly, so patiently, and all alone?

Time is the great unraveller of mysteries.

And, therefore, we must leave this mystery to the sure solution of the course of time.

CHAPTER XXVI.

The beginning of the serenade.

PATIENTLY the mysterious figure kept up its solitary watch. Minute sped after minute, the unclouded moon now shed its radiance full upon the closed and silent houses, and upon the lonely street, deserted save by a chance pedestrian or a solitary wagon. And all this time, with every fitful breeze, the old tin sign kept up its melancholic and spasmodic music. And all this time that strange, dark spot lay upon the pavement, a weird shadow without motion and without change.

At length, from a great distance, came a faint sound as of the tramp of several feet. The figure instantly started into an attitude of keen and eager watchfulness, and peered cautiously over the fence in the direction from which the sounds proceeded. He was not kept long in suspense, for the sound of approaching feet grew gradually louder, soon a number of dark forms could be seen approaching, then followed the hum of voices, and a few minutes later several dark shadows passed him, immediately followed by the owners of the shadows themselves.

There were eight individuals who thus passed before the sharp scrutinizing gaze of the unsuspected watcher. They advanced until they reached the house before which the despondent sign greeted them with its rasping, nerve-grating welcome, and here they halted upon a signal from the first man, who was none other than Mr. Cliphart, which gave the last man, Mr. Brankey, who, in a partially inebriated state had found it somewhat difficult to keep up with his more sober companions, an opportunity to rest his weary and unreliable limbs by taking a seat upon the wooden steps before the professor's door. The other six men who had advanced, sandwiched, as it were, between Mr. Cliphart and Mr. Brankey, were the musicians who had been hired to awaken the echoes of the silent street at this unusual hour in honor of the gentle Bella.

Having thus arrived at their destination, the leader took from his coffin-like box a violin, an example which his five companions instantly followed by likewise producing their particular instruments of music.

One — a short chubby gentleman, with exceedingly fat cheeks — drew from some hidden receptacle in the inside of his coat a cornet. Another — a gray-headed gentleman in a blue blouse — opened a coffin-like box similar to the leader's and also produced therefrom a violin. A third — a young, brawny, broad-shouldered fellow, whose hands looked more fit to wield the blacksmith's hammer, stripped the bag from his guitar and suspended the instrument by a ribbon across his shoulder. The fourth — an exceedingly stout German in spectacles, whose clothes were so tight that they seemed to be in constant danger of bursting at the seams, produced from several pockets the various parts of a flute and put them together, while the fifth — a pale, delicate youth, in an immense hat and garments that might have been made for his neighbor, the German, brought, from the depths of an enormous pocket, a triangle.

"Is it all ready, yentlemans?" inquired Mr. Cliphart.

"It is all ready," replied the leader.

"Naw, den, gif uns someting goot. Bella is en goot girl," explained Mr. Cliphart.

"All right, my hearty," said the dapper leader,

"we'll give her 'Nellie Gray.' Now then, one, two, three!"

And then in a burst of the most wonderful discord the silence of that quiet street was broken, and the great serenade began.

CHAPTER XXVII.

The wonderful serenade.

OF all the singular, ear-piercing, wonderful, excruciating sounds which have startled a long-suffering humanity under the guise and pretence of music, these which burst forth under the mournful sign and utterly drowned the creakings and the wailings of that melancholic article, most certainly bore off the palm.

As the misguided French perpetrated the wildest excesses under the sacred name of Liberty, so these deluded amateurs imposed upon the startled neighborhood a medley of the most outrageous noises under the honored name of music.

Not only was each instrument seized with an intense desire to make as much noise as it possibly could, but it appeared to be infused with the belief that it was not under the least obligation to play in time or tune with any other.

Wherefore, there arose a succession of the most heart-rending discords that the world has ever heard.

The violins, especially, appeared to have concentrated all the rival jealousies and spites that have afflicted those famous instruments through their owners since the days of Paganini, and played in such an inexcusably inharmonious and obstinate manner that it is a wonder that all the cats and dogs in the neighborhood did not burst forth in one simultaneous and unearthly howl.

The triangle jingled along at the same rate without a pause and without any reference whatever to time or propriety, and rivalled the efforts of any lusty child of three in possession of a spoon and a tin pan. In consequence of the flute struggling along a note or two behind the others the peculiar effect of that instrument upon that glorious concert can better be imagined than described. The cornet was no better, and caused its possessor, the short, chubby gentleman with the fat cheeks, to perform the most ridiculous antics — now blowing with might and main until his eyes were almost closed by his puffed-out cheeks, then doubling up as if in intense pain and suddenly straightening out again, with perspiration on his brow and exhaustion written all over his face — the sole result of these extraordinary efforts being that the cornet never produced a note at the right time, but came in with the most appalling

THE SERENADE.— Page 262.

sounds when it was the last thing that should have been heard.

But the truthful chronicler must acknowledge, albeit with regret and pain, that of all the humbugs, frauds and impostors with which the musical world has been afflicted, the guitar must certainly be ranked as chief and foremost. How the young man who carried that much abused instrument had ever conceived the idea that violently scraping the strings with the knuckles of his right hand without a pause for ten minutes at a time could ever produce sounds bearing even the remotest resemblance to any kind of music, is entirely beyond our comprehension. But that he did assiduously continue this exercise, we are loth to say, cannot be denied.

While this incomparable serenade was at its very height there approached from the direction opposite to the one from which the serenaders had come, four individuals, who, when they reached the corner of the street nearest to Professor Bulbous' house, stopped and contemplated the scene before them with great interest and attention.

"Bob," said Harry, for these newcomers were none other than Uncle Dan and his youthful friends, "what do you think of that?"

"Think!" cried Bob, explosively; for that young

gentleman was highly indignant that the lady of his affections should be favored with such a night-tearing performance, "think! I don't *think* at all. I *know* that this is the most outrageous noise I ever heard. I'd like to kick those fellows into — into —— "

"The middle of next week," smilingly suggested Mr. Doolittle.

"Well, you can laugh as much as you please. I think it's an outrage on the community. They ought to be lynched!"

"Dear me!" exclaimed Uncle Dan, "don't get angry, Bob."

"Look!" cried Harry, who had been laughing immoderately, "the people are getting excited. There'll be a bombardment with wash-basins and bootjacks pretty soon."

"Well, I think there ought to be," said the aggrieved Mr. Sturdy.

"Oh, no, Bob," soothingly remarked Uncle Dan, "don't be harsh."

It was true that the peculiar music was beginning to attract unusual attention; for the windows of many of the neighboring houses were beginning to open, and as the blinds were thrown back several white-robed figures could be seen looking anxiously out.

The attention of the four friends was here attracted by a wonderful burst from the serenading party which quite eclipsed all previous efforts, and which would have had precisely the same effect upon a person of musical taste as the action of drawing a rusty nail back and forth between a set of closed teeth. During this unequalled effort the short, chubby little gentleman was seen to bend down almost to the pavement, and then suddenly arise and spring a foot from the ground, in the intense agony of trying to produce a sound from the cornet; whereupon Mr. Cribbler, whose sense of the ridiculous was thereby keenly excited, found it necessary to clasp an awning-post for support, while even the usually undemonstrative Mr. Doolittle laughed outright.

"Horrible!" said Mr. Sturdy, shaking his fist, "I wonder the police don't come and arrest the whole set. The professor ought to drive them away from the house."

"Bob," entreated Uncle Dan, "I beg of you, be more calm."

Doubtless it cannot be denied that the greatest efforts sometimes remain unrewarded. And so it proved in this instance. For in the professor's house not a door turned upon its hinges, not a shutter was opened, not a window was raised; all was dark and silent as if there was not a human being in the house, and to all appearances the serenaders would have been equally successful if they had delivered their touching strains before a building upon whose wall was pasted the short but touching phrase, "For Rent."

So Mr. Cliphart evidently thought; though by what process of reasoning that usually slow-witted individual arrived at this conclusion it has not been possible to discover. But that he did make up his mind to this effect we must believe, since no sooner had the last ear-piercing, aggravating sound with its attendant echoes died away, than Mr. Cliphart, inserting the middle fingers of his hands into the corners of his mouth, gave vent to a whistle, which was so keen, so shrill, so cutting, long and loud that it quite outrivalled any instrument in the whole collection in its wildest rendition.

"Oh!" screamed Mr. Cribbler. And then Mr. Cribbler grasped the awning-post affectionately once more, shook his head helplessly, allowed the tears to roll unchecked out of his eyes, assumed a scarlet complexion, laughed until he coughed, coughed until he choked, and choked until he looked like a wilted red cabbage.

Uncle Dan favored the musicians with open-eyed and open-mouthed regards, too astonished even to relieve his mind with his customary "Dear me!" Bob found it necessary to sit down on a flour barrel, which lay conveniently near, and beat an exciting tattoo with his heels against the barrel-head, while Dick thrust his hands down into his pockets, threw back his head, and roared aloud.

"Man alive!" cried the leader of the musicians, placing his hand upon Mr. Cliphart's arm, and thus intercepting another echo-producing whistle, "what do you mean by that? What in the world are you doing that for?"

"Naw," retorted Mr. Cliphart, in an injured tone, "why sa not comen?"

"Tha's what I say," assented Mr. Brankey, from the steps, "wha's use stayin' 'ere all night?"

As if in answer to this question the shutters near Mr. Brankey's head were suddenly and violently thrown open, and the light of a coal-oil lamp, pouring through the window, outlined the burly form of the professor.

CHAPTER XXVIII.

Which is chiefly remarkable, as showing Mr. Brankey's great respect for Professor Bulbous, as presenting Mr. Cliphart in the rôle of a peacemaker, and as dissolving a mysterious shadow into equally mysterious flame.

OW," growled the professor, in a remarkably gruff tone of voice, "what's the matter out here?"

Professor Bulbous' clothes appeared to have been hastily thrown on, his hair was frowsy, and he was devoid of coat, collar, or necktie. This sight, added to the gruff tone of his voice and the uninviting nature of his question, was an unexpected damper upon the ardor of the serenaders, and no one ventured to reply.

"I ask," broke forth the professor, with increasing severity, "what is the matter out here? What is all this noise about?"

"We really beg your pardon," said the leader of the orchestra, in a tone of the most scrupulous and conciliatory politeness, "if our music has disturbed you. But the truth is, we came to pay our respects to your beautiful and accomplished daughter."

"Huh!" grunted the professor. "I dare say! The girl is in bed, and I don't want her to be excited by any such nonsense. Gentlemen, I am much obliged to you, but the music has been quite sufficient. Good night!" And so saying, the professor stretched out his hand to close the shutters. But at that moment his eyes fell upon Mr. Brankey, who was at that moment furtively turning down the rim of his hat in the endeavor to make himself unrecognizable.

Pushing back the shutter which he had partially closed, the professor placed his two broad hands upon the window-sill, and projecting himself half way out of the window, said, in a stern voice,— "Brankey, is that you?"

It would have done any one good to have seen Mr. Brankey pull his hat down over his eyes and shrink into the smallest possible compass, as if by this ostrich-like proceeding to avoid the keen and searching glance of the professor. But the professor, as may readily be supposed, was not to be fooled by any such ridiculous performance.

"Brankey," growled the professor in his gruffest tones, "if you are sober enough to answer me, I want to know what you mean by coming here at this time of night and rousing honest folks out of bed."

Here Mr. Cliphart came bravely to the rescue of his friend, and drew upon himself the ire of the burly musician.

"Naw, professore," said Mr. Cliphart, "you mus'n' getten mat."

The professor turned his attention to the large-featured gentleman who had thus addressed him. and angrily demanded, "Who are you, sir?"

"Naw, professore," said Mr. Cliphart, with a deprecating wave of his huge right hand, "dat is nix. Wat makes dat out? But you mus'n' getten mat."

"I am not accustomed to dictation, sir," said the professor, with lofty scorn, "and I don't want to hear any more of it, sir."

"Yaw, professore — dat is yust right. But make it not en liddle too bat."

"Well, move on, sir. Take your crew away. Move along!"

"Naw, why schull I moven? You mus'n' getten mat. Let uns play en liddle mooseek."

This refusal to leave the premises, and the repetition of Mr. Cliphart's advice, so enraged the professor that he hastily withdrew from the window with an ominous, "I'll see whether you won't move along, sir," and immediately reappeared at the door. Descending the stairs without noticing Mr. Brankey, who trembled in his boots, the professor approached Mr. Cliphart, and in a threatening tone demanded, —

"Will you move along, sir?" and waited for an answer.

That answer never came. The black shadow which had lain so long and so immovably upon the moonlit pavement, moved at last, not through the changes of the moon, but through the agency of quite another power. No one, apparently, saw the dark figure hiding behind the fence slowly bend down, or saw the flickering little blaze of a match as it approached the end of the trail that led from the shadow. In the next instant there was a line of light which crept swiftly to the black spot upon the pavement, and suddenly the whole dark shadow burst into a wild red sheet of flame that entirely enveloped the professor and Mr. Cliphart in its fiery folds.

But, fierce and high as had been the flame it vanished in a moment, leaving the musicians thoroughly awe-struck and bewildered.

Fortunately no person's clothing was set on fire by the mysterious blaze, and, consequently, any serious consequences were averted. But blinded, scorched, stunned, and astonished, the professor staggered back, and in so doing knocked the dazed Mr. Brankey from his perch upon the stairs, whereupon that gentleman rolled into the corner between the stairs and the wall of the house and lay there in his clouded helplessness powerless to rise.

Mr. Cliphart was not only blinded, scorched, stunned, and astonished, but in addition to these effects he was also frightened out of his wits. For, to this gentleman's rather dull perceptions, the fire seemed to have flashed suddenly out of the very earth beneath him ; and, without stopping to consider whether it was traceable to any earthly origin, Mr. Cliphart, horror stricken and alarmed, imagined himself a prey to supernatural fire, and felt convinced that a terrible disaster was about to overtake him.

"Wa-ater ! wa-ater!" cried the thoroughly frightened man, "wa-ater ! I is on de fire ! Putta me out ! Putta me out !" and, without waiting for anybody to comply with this unnecessary request, Mr. Cliphart ambled homewards, making the quiet streets re-echo with cries for "Wa-ater !" and earnest requests for somebody to " Putta me out ! "

As the professor slowly recovered from his bewilderment, the wise musicians, acting upon that old, respectable, and exceedingly convenient saying, "Discretion is the better part of valor," quietly withdrew and soon were out of sight. At the same time a groan from Mr. Brankey betrayed him, and drew upon his devoted head the concentrated wrath and vengeance of the now angry professor. Grasping him by the collar, Professor Bulbous brought Mr. Brankey up from the obscurity of his corner with a sudden and powerful jerk, and, taking a firm hold with both hands, gave the poor man such an unmerciful shaking, that Bob, Dick, Harry and Uncle Dan felt strongly tempted to interfere.

Indeed, they were upon the point of doing so, when the professor, with one final effort, shook Mr. Brankey into the gutter and left him there, and then hastily ascending the stairs, disappeared into the house without stopping to discover the cause of the mysterious flame.

"Dear me!" said Uncle Dan, "dear me! What sights! And there lies Mr. Brankey again unable to help himself. Poor fellow! Come, let us help him to his feet and take him home."

And this kindly act was accordingly duly performed by Uncle Dan, Mr. Sturdy, and Mr. Cribbler. But Mr. Doolittle was gone. He had not said "good-bye," and no one knew when or how he had left them. And thus ended the great, the unrivalled, the exciting serenade. Not a single person present had seen Miss Bella Bulbous. But Miss Bella Bulbous, peeping through the shutters, had seen every individual member of the company and witnessed all that had transpired.

CHAPTER XXIX.

Uncle Dan prepares to receive expected visitors· and receives two who were not expected.

UPON the following day, Uncle Dan, still filled with astonishment at the wonderful scene he had witnessed, and having racked his brain all night in vain for a plausible solution of the enigma, and having bothered Aunt Prudence with all sorts of impossible theories until that worthy lady peremptorily forbade any further allusion to the subject, decided to invite his young friends to take tea with him, and around the festive board talk over the exciting events that had occurred.

Uncle Dan never did anything by halves. Wherefore, when it was actually arranged with Aunt Prudence's gracious permission that his young friends were to visit him upon the succeeding evening, he rushed out of the house, and hurrying to various grocers, bakers and confectioners, sent home such an abundance of edibles and sweetmeats that more conservative Aunt Prudence wondered whether her excellent spouse was in his right mind.

"What in the world that man wants me to do with all these things," thought Aunt Prudence with a ludicrous glance of dismay at a barrel of apples, a box of oranges, another of lemons, a keg of cider and a dozen pies, with cakes *ad infinitum*, which formed the first instalment of Uncle Dan's hospitable impulse, "I can't for the life of me imagine."

It having been decided that Miss Wright should also be one of the guests, Uncle Dan had dismissed her as early as three o'clock, under the vague impression that a young lady's preparations for a visit of this kind were necessarily so complicated and elaborate that four hours were short enough to devote to such an important work.

The evening came, but Dick was missing. Dick had promised to call for Uncle Dan, not later than seven o'clock, at the store. And now it was half-past the hour and no Dick had arrived. Uncle Dan grew momentarily more uneasy, and as the clock struck eight he found the suspense unbearable, and determined, in his impulsive manner, to take a turn or two in the neighborhood to see if he could not meet Mr. Doolittle and somewhat accelerate that dilatory young gentleman's steps.

Putting on his hat, and telling Jimmy to "send Mr. Doolittle up to the house at once if he should come in, and close the store at nine o'clock," Uncle Dan approached the door with an undefined determination to find Dick by walking up one street and down another. But this commendable determination was destined to fail of accomplishment. For scarcely had Uncle Dan started toward the door when there entered a lady and gentleman.

Uncle Dan stopped and favored tne couple with an inquiring glance through his spectacles. His face was instantly illuminated by one of his broadest smiles, and in a tone of the heartiest welcome, he cried out, " Mr. Brock! Miss Brock! How do you do? Dear me! I am delighted to see you. Come in, come right in."

" Mr. Poldertot, I am fortunate in finding you," said Mr. Brock, shaking hands warmly with Uncle Dan, " I feared you had gone home."

"Dear me! Dear me!" exclaimed Uncle Dan, as he placed chairs and motioned his visitors to sit down, " you were lucky. For, as you see, I was on the point of going out."

" Do not let me detain you," said Mr. Brock,— "don't stop on our account."

"Oh, I had no particular business," Uncle Dan

hastened to say. "When did you come to town, Mr. Brock?"

"We came, sir," replied the squire, "about an hour ago. We came here as soon as we could find your address."

"Thank you, thank you," said Uncle Dan, much pleased. And then he added in a lower tone, "And I hope you come to bring me good news. I hope you have come to tell me that your daughter has been found."

A shadow appeared in the squire's face, and tears started to the eyes of his fair companion.

"I have not found her, sir."

"Dear me! Dear me!" said Uncle Dan, with sorrowful sympathy, "And have you learned nothing at all about her?"

"Nothing directly — nothing reliable — " said the squire, sadly.

"You know," said Miss Brock, looking wistfully at Uncle Dan, "that your friend Mr. Doolittle has been so kind as to assist us in the search, and we had a note from him, which, without giving us any information, led us to hope that we might soon be able to learn something by coming here."

"Dear me!" was all that Uncle Dan could say.

"Whether that is possible or not," said Mr. Brock, "I can only say, sir, that I cannot remain idle at home while the search is carried on by others. I *must* and *will* find my daughter. I drove her away——"

"Gently — gently," said Uncle Dan.

"I did, sir; it almost drives me wild when I think of it. I made home a place of torment to her. I shut her out of my love. I tried to force her to do what she can never and ought never to do. Oh, how blind I was! And now she haunts me every day. I see her in the night and hear her calling me. She comes to me in dreams and beckons to me until I start up in the darkness, beside myself with fear and grief, imagining all sorts of dangers and horrors that may surround her. And so I have left the house, not to return until I find my daughter."

The squire was greatly agitated, and Miss Brock was weeping, a sight that stirred Uncle Dan's easily-touched sympathies to their deepest depths.

"Let me assure you, sir," said the kindest-hearted of human beings, "that you have my fullest sympathy; and that my assistance at any time is cheerfully yours."

"Sir," said Squire Brock, "I can only thank you, and prove that I am grateful, by accepting your assistance whenever you can help me."

"I am glad you came to-day," said Uncle Dan,

"for this very evening there is to be a little gathering at my house for tea, and Mr. Doolittle is among the number whom I expect to see there. And if you have no special engagement, I would be delighted to have you, sir, and Miss Brock accompany me home, and then you can talk your plans over together."

"Thank you, sir," replied Mr. Brock, "but my daughter and I would not like to intrude our sorrow upon such an occasion."

"Intrude!" cried Uncle Dan, "Dear me! What do you mean? Don't say that again. I feel like thanking you for paying me this visit, and here you come talking about intrusion! Dear me! Dear me! Not another word, sir. Not another word. Jimmy, don't forget what I told you about Dick. Send him up to the house immediately, if he comes here. Now, Miss Brock — my arm. Thank you. Here we go, all pleasant and comfortable, and if we don't make Aunt Prudence open her eyes then snow doesn't fall in December."

And in this hearty manner did Uncle Dan overcome the scruples of his guests, and lead them through the dark streets to his hospitable home.

CHAPTER XXX.

The inexplicable absence of Mr. Richard Doolittle continues; and, on the contrary, Mr. William Bromley and Mr. Ben Seldon put in an appearance in their usual quiet and harmonious manner. — A summons for Aunt Prudence. — A very unsatisfactory tea.

CHEERILY the lights shone in Uncle Dan's modest little room; the furniture dusted and rubbed and polished by Aunt Prudence's busy hands looked like new; even the pictures had received an extra rubbing, and looked as if they had just been hung upon the walls; and as for the carpets, let it simply be said, that Aunt Prudence had swept them twice, and every one will know that the effort to find a speck of dust or a stray bit of thread upon them would have been a hopeless task, indeed. The very tins in the kitchen shone at each other with extraordinary brightness, and the table-ware on the dining-room table — for Aunt Prudence was prepared and waiting for her guests — was so clean and inviting that she gave the table-cloth a final rub with both hands and favored the cups and saucers with an approving little nod, as if to say, "I think you will do." And when Aunt Prudence intimated anything of the kind, you may be sure that it was strictly and entirely true. Having thus silently expressed her opinion of her own work, she entered the sitting-room, and taking up her knitting from the table, fell busily to work, and rocked herself gently to and fro in the rocking-chair. When Aunt Prudence had nothing else to do she knitted. And any one who knew her also knew that knitting was to Aunt Prudence both rest and recreation.

Thus in busy silence an hour had passed away. An hour during which nothing could be heard but the clicking of the needles, the ticking of the clock, and drowsy humming of the jolly little kettle on the kitchen stove.

The quiet of this comfortable scene was at length broken by the ringing of the door-bell — so unmistakably the gentle "ting-a-ling" with which Uncle Dan usually sought admittance that Aunt Prudence laid aside her knitting with slow deliberation, and then approached the door with a countenance that would have caused considerable apprehension in Uncle Dan's mind had he seen it.

"Now," thought Aunt Prudence, "I'll find out what Daniel meant by sending home a whole wagon load of provisions — some of them sure to spoil or get stale before we can eat them all — as if we are going to start a hotel."

And with this thought Aunt Prudence turned the latch, and, with a sudden pull, opened the door. Now, it so happened that Uncle Dan was quite thoughtlessly and carelessly leaning against the door, having turned to say a word to his guest, Mr. Brock. And when the door was thus suddenly opened, Uncle Dan, being suddenly deprived of his support, tottered back, tripped on the door-sill, and, finally, overcome by the attraction of gravitation, sat down at his good wife's feet with a jar that shook the whole house and caused him to ejaculate "Dear me!" with more than usual force and expression.

"Ha!" said Aunt Prudence, bending over her husband with a look of stern displeasure, "is this the condition you come home in?"

"Dear me!" exclaimed Uncle Dan. Then he scrambled to his feet. "Dear me!" he said again, and looked ruefully at the place where he had fallen. "Dear me!" he said for the third time, as he began to brush his clothes with his hands, "how could you open the door so quickly, Prudence?"

"And how could you come home in such a condition that you needed a door to lean against?"

retorted Aunt Prudence, with cutting scorn, "Doors are made to be opened occasionally, I believe, and not altogether to hold up men who are not ——"

"My dear Prudence," interrupted Uncle Dan, with evident pain, "you certainly would not accuse me of ——"

"I don't accuse you of anything," said Aunt Prudence, "but if I had brought a lady and gentleman to my house I would invite them to come in, and not keep them waiting at the door all night."

"Dear me!" said poor Uncle Dan, painfully conscience-stricken, "how very stupidly forgetful I am! I beg a thousand pardons. Come in — come in. Prudence, Mr. Brock — Miss Brock — Mrs. Poldertot."

The door was closed and they passed into the cozy little parlor.

"I hope," said Aunt Prudence, in almost the same words used by Uncle Dan, "that you have come with good news."

"On the contrary," replied Mr. Brock, "it is in the hope of hearing good news that we are here to-night."

At this moment Mr. Cribbler and Mr. Sturdy arrived, and were warmly received by Uncle Dan and introduced to the unexpected visitors.

"And so they concluded, my dear, you see," said Uncle Dan, addressing his wife, when Mr. Sturdy had made a most stately bow, and Mr. Cribbler had smiled in his most fascinating manner, and both had seated themselves upon the sofa — "to pay us a visit."

"In this conclusion," added Squire Brock (the title of Squire had been acquired by virtue of his office as Justice), "we have been influenced by the receipt of a note from Mr. Doolittle, who holds out some slight hope of being able to give us information that may interest us."

"And you may be sure," said Uncle Dan, smiling, "that Dick would never have sent you such a message unless he had something worth telling."

"Not a doubt about it," asserted Mr. Sturdy, in his usual positive tone, and checking off the sentence with a sweep of his little forefinger, "not a single solitary doubt."

The conversation continued for a quarter of an hour, Uncle Dan all the while growing more and more impatient at the continued absence of Dick and Miss Wright. And he had even made up his mind to run over to Mrs. Bromley's, which was in the next block, to see what could delay the young lady so long, when there suddenly arose a loud and unusual noise, which began at the bottom of the back stairs, and increased in power and volume as it ascended, until it culminated in a series of deafening knocks, like the attack of three or four weighty sledge-hammers upon the door.

"Dear me!" said Uncle Dan, starting from his chair, "what's that?"

Then followed an extraordinary tumult, during which a high voice could be heard as of one who was getting the worst of it.

"Oh! Oh! Let go my nose — deal with me gently — spare my young heart — ouch! my ears — a little longer lease of life — stay, jailer, stay — Oh, let up, Bill. Enough's enough."

"I'll let you up," growled a heavy voice in reply, "I'll give you enough! Punch me with a lath again when I'm going up-stairs, will you? Pull up one of my feet before I put down the other, will you? I'll lath you! I'll pull up your feet for you! For two cents I'd pitch you over the railing."

"Can't do it — only one cent left," said the high voice, "you borrowed all the rest and haven't paid it back. Oh, so gently o'er me stealing — that'll do, William — let dogs delight to bark and bite — and — oh — ouch — oh-h-h!"

"I steal, do I? I'm a dog, am I? I bark and bite, do I? I'll show you!"

Then arose another uproar, followed by the noise of a fall, and succeeded by another series of sledge-hammer-like blows upon the door.

"Dear me!" ejaculated Uncle Dan, as the truth dawned upon him, "that must be Mr. Bromley and Mr. Seldon."

"And if you don't want them to break down the door and alarm all the neighbors, you had better see what they want," observed Aunt Prudence.

"Dear me! so I had — so I had," said Uncle Dan, and, approaching the door, threw it wide open; whereupon there stood revealed the burly form, tangled hair, and frowning face of Mr. Bromley, while the lighter form of Mr. Seldon could be seen in the background just rising from a prostrate position on the porch.

Mr. Bromley's trousers were tucked into his boot-tops, his coat sleeves were rolled up to his elbows, and his cap, as usual, occupied a precarious position upon the back of his head. Thus Mr. Bromley asserted his independence of the stale conventionalities of life.

"How do you do, William?" said Uncle Dan, cordially. "Come in."

"No," said Mr. Bromley, with gruff brevity, "I won't do it. I want to see Aunt Prudence."

"Well, my dear fellow," said Uncle Dan, pleasantly, "she is in the house. Step in — do."

"No," said Mr. Bromley again, "I won't do it. Tell her to come here."

And as Mr. Bromley peremptorily refused to enter the house, Uncle Dan was perforce obliged to ask Aunt Prudence to go to the door.

"Why don't he come in?" asked Aunt Prudence.

"I'm sure I don't know," said Uncle Dan.

"I have half a mind not to see him, the noisy fellow!"

Nevertheless, Aunt Prudence arose and advanced toward the obnoxious young man.

In a few moments she returned with a strange expression on her face.

"Mrs. Bromley has sent for me, Daniel," she said, "and I will have to go. I will return, I hope, in a short time."

"What!" cried Uncle Dan. "Is anything the matter with Miss Wright?"

"Something *is* the matter with Miss Wright," said Aunt Prudence, significantly.

"Oh, dear! oh, dear!" exclaimed Uncle Dan, with a look and tone of great apprehension; "I was afraid of it. She's been run over, or knocked down or robbed, or had a fit, or —— "

"Nothing of the kind," said Aunt Prudence. "You will know all about it in good time. Mr. Brock and Miss Brock will, I am sure, excuse me, as the call is urgent."

"Certainly, certainly," said Mr. Brock.

"Daniel, the tea is all ready, and you had better invite our friends to the table. I shall not be gone long, I think, but we cannot tell what may happen. So go right to the table and don't wait for me. And don't spill any tea on the table-cloth."

And with this parting injunction, Aunt Prudence left her perplexed and anxious husband to entertain his guests, while she descended the stairs and advanced along the street towards Mrs. Bromley's house, having first discreetly placed herself between Mr. Bromley and Mr. Seldon, and taken an arm of each, thereby effectually preventing, for the time being, that vivacious warfare in which these heroes were constantly engaged.

CHAPTER XXXI.

The success of Mr. Doolittle's endeavors. — The lost found. — And the extraordinary antics indulged in upon this occasion by the overjoyed Mr. Poldertot.

THE time passed very slowly in Uncle Dan's parlor, or, as he modestly termed it, his front room, where, after the uncomfortable supper was over, Uncle Dan sat with his guests and awaited Aunt Prudence's return.

"It seems to me," said Mr. Brock, at length, "that anything would be easier to bear than this suspense. It is terrible. This inaction is very hard to endure."

"Courage," said Uncle Dan, cheerfully, "courage. Everything happens for the best."

"I don't doubt it," said Mr. Brock, gloomily, "when a man's arm is amputated to save his life it happens for the best; but the loss and the pain are not the less hard to bear."

"The greater hero he," said Uncle Dan, "who bears them cheerfully and well."

"You are right," replied Mr. Brock, "and I will endeavor to be patient. But I long to hear from my dear girl, and if any one is now upon the way to bring me tidings, I hope the messenger will soon appear."

"The messenger is here!"

It was a familiar voice that spoke. They started and looked around. And before the door which he had closed behind him stood Mr. Dick Doolittle. He had entered noiselessly and unperceived from the sitting-room, and now stood with his hat under his arm and his hands clasped behind him, and looked like a sociably-inclined neighbor who might have come in to play a game of checkers or dominoes with Uncle Dan.

"Dick, my dear boy," exclaimed Uncle Dan, rising in haste and advancing with a beaming smile, "I'm overjoyed to see you. Dear me! Why did you not come sooner? Have you seen Prudence? And can you tell me what is the matter with Miss Wright?"

Dick advanced into the centre of the room and greeted Uncle Dan's guests, who, in their excitement, had arisen and were anxiously waiting to hear the news, placed his hat upon a book-shelf, and, turning to Uncle Dan, said gravely, —

"Uncle Dan, you asked me whether I had seen Aunt Prudence. Yes, I have. What is the matter with Miss Wright? Miss Wright is no more."

Uncle Dan looked horror-struck.

"You misunderstood me," said Dick. "Miss Wright is not dead."

"Dear me!" exclaimed the easily perplexed Uncle Dan, "I never can understand you, my boy, when you speak in enigmas. I suppose you will make it all clear. Only remember, Dick, that our friends here are longing to hear about their lost one, and if you know anything about her tell it right away, my boy, tell it right away."

There was a strange light in Dick's eyes, and a new expression in his usually passive face, as he looked across the table at the squire and said, slowly and distinctly, "Mr. Brock, your daughter is found."

Mr. Brock bowed his head in silent gratitude, tears came into Miss Brock's eyes, and neither could trust themselves to speak.

As for Uncle Dan, the beaming smile upon his ruddy face, the joyful tears that glistened through his spectacles, and which he vainly endeavored to hide by winking a great many times with extraordinary rapidity, and his half open mouth, were proof positive that the very depths of his sympathetic heart were touched.

"Uncle Dan has in his employ a young lady whom we call Miss Wright," began Dick.

"Quite right, quite right," said Uncle Dan, "and she ought to have been here this evening."

Dick smiled and went on. As briefly as possible, for he was never known to waste any words, Dick told the story of his discovery of Miss Brock. How being frequently in Uncle Dan's store he had seen Miss Wright, and, being struck with the mystery that surrounded her former life, had watched her more closely than he might otherwise have done. How, when Joel Krowps had given him the photograph, he saw that the features resembled Miss Wright's, and he determined to discover, if possible, without alarming the lady, whether she was the lost daughter or not. How he had sought in vain for proof, not desiring, on the one hand, to appear unduly inquisitive about Miss Wright's affairs, nor, on the other hand, to raise hopes which might lead to disappointment. How, finally, he had determined, finding no other way to solve the mystery, to induce Squire Brock to come to the city with a view to bringing him, as if by accident, face to face with the lady, and had for this reason written to the squire. How that the discovery which he hoped to make had been brought about in quite another way. And in this way, namely: that, passing Mrs. Bromley's house that evening on his way to Uncle Dan's, he was astonished to hear Mrs. Bromley calling him, and, in an agitated voice, inviting him to enter. That he had done so, when Mrs. Bromley had begged him, with tears in her eyes, to see Miss Wright and say something to her, because she would not listen to Mrs. Bromley at all, but was packing her trunk in a state of great alarm and agitation, with the evident intention of going away at once, Heaven knew where, and would give no explanation of her extraordinary conduct. That Dick had accordingly waited until Miss Wright had come hurriedly down the stairs to leave the house. Feeling that the time had come for him to act, for, if she disappeared now, he might never find her again, he had suddenly confronted her in the hall at the foot of the stairs. She had tried to pass him, demanding, indignantly, to know why he presumed to stop her.

Another course might have been better, but at the moment none occurred to him. He took the photograph Joel had given him from his pocket, and holding it out, said, —

"That is my right and my apology."

That the shock of being thus suddenly apprised that she was known, for it was indeed Miss Brock, had unnerved her, and she would have fallen had he not supported her. That they carried her into a room and laid her on the sofa, and worked to revive her. That she had only recovered from one swoon to fall into another, until becoming alarmed, especially as Mrs. Bromley appeared to be becoming quite helpless and hysterical herself, he had sent for Aunt Prudence and a physician. And that, he was happy to say, with these two efficient aids, she had rapidly recovered her composure. And that when this had been accomplished, finding further concealment impossible, she had freely confessed, and had also made known the cause of her singular agitation and alarm, which was simply the fact that Mr. Rolf Seppeld had accidentally met her on the street and penetrated her disguise, and then, calling her by name, had stopped and threatened to expose her unless she consented to go back to her father's house with him.

"And that's all," says Dick.

Frequently during this recital, Dick had stopped as if to listen. And now, when the story has been told, he goes to the door and looks out.

"May Heaven reward him," says Mr. Brock, " I never can."

Miss Brock is silently weeping, and Uncle Dan's eyes are so full of tears that he can only wink now at rare intervals.

At this moment there is heard a light step and the rustle of a dress. Dick opens the door wider.

What is it that causes Miss Brock to spring to her feet with a cry of joy? What makes Squire Brock rush forward with open arms?

A face of mingled shame and happiness — a form of grace and loveliness — a pair of large bright eyes suffused with tears. There is a laugh and a cry — a sob and a sound of joy — then the words, uttered with a world of passionate yearning and unfailing love, —

"Father — oh, father!"

"My daughter! My daughter!"

And the lost child is folded once more to the hearts that have mourned her loss and longed for her return. Uncle Dan, Dick, Harry, and Bob quietly leave the room and close the door behind them. Whereupon they find themselves before prim, stiff, upright, but nevertheless kindly-hearted Aunt Prudence.

"Well!" says Aunt Prudence.

"Well!" exclaims Uncle Dan.

And then, suddenly obeying an irresistible impulse, that overjoyed gentleman puts his right arm around his stately partner's waist, waves his left arm wildly in the air, and, with a "Hip! hip!

UNCLE DAN SHOCKS AUNT PRUDENCE.— Page 296.

hurrah!" goes circling frantically around the room, while Aunt Prudence, without breath to say a word, can only stare over her husband's shoulder with an inexpressible look of astonishment and dismay.

CHAPTER XXXII.

In which some matters that have hitherto been secrets are explained. — A startling appeal.

IT was with a heavy heart that Uncle Dan, in company with Dick, returned to his humble home upon the following evening, after having witnessed the safe departure of the reunited family from the railroad depot.

"For," explained Mr. Poldertot, "I feel as if I had lost a daughter; I do, indeed."

Having thus expressed himself, Uncle Dan sank into a chair, and, placing the broad palms of his hands over his stout knees, favored his better-half, and his young friend with a prolonged stare.

"I cannot understand," said Aunt Prudence, "how any man could treat his daughter so unjustly. If what she told me is true, he acted like a regular bear."

"Well, well," said Uncle Dan, softly, "everything is forgotten and forgiven, my dear, forgotten and forgiven."

"He actually kept her locked up in her room, and she only escaped by accident," pursued Aunt Prudence.

"Can that be possible!" exclaimed the shocked Mr. Poldertot.

"Oh, yes," said Dick; "quite true. Squire Brock is subject to fits of uncontrollable temper, which, at times, almost reach the height of temporary insanity."

"But I cannot understand," Aunt Prudence went on to say, with immeasurable scorn and indignation compressed into the tones of her voice, "how *that Seppeld* could have acquired such an influence over Mr. Brock."

"Money," said Dick, sententiously.

"Ah!"

"Yes: told Brock he was rich; the squire needed money — he's deeply in debt — although he has a fine property; thought it would be a fine thing to have a rich son-in-law; Seppeld promised to pay his debts as soon as he married the girl — the girl wouldn't do it. That's all."

"And so it was to be a regular bargain and sale," was Aunt Prudence's comment. "Well, all I can say is, I'm glad he has come to his senses."

"Is Mr. Seppeld so rich?" inquired Uncle Dan.

"Poor as a church mouse," said Dick.

"Dear me! Then what made him so persistent in his addresses to Miss Brock?"

"Money," said Dick, again.

"Ah!" said Aunt Prudence once more.

"Yes; he thought the squire was rich — fine property, at least. He would marry the girl — get hold of the property — get rid of the girl afterwards. It was a deep game. He's sharp. As to the squire's debts — they didn't trouble him — debts never do."

"I see," said Uncle Dan, "how weak we are to resist temptation! I am sorry for the young man."

"Oh, of course!" observed Aunt Prudence, sarcastically, "I never knew you to hear of a rogue that you wasn't sorry for."

"My dear," said Uncle Dan, "let us not be too hasty in condemning. Some of us are like iron and some like lead; and fire will melt one quicker than another; but iron will break when lead will only bend. Trials and temptations may come to us all: and the one who will resist — who knows? who knows?"

"By which you mean that if I was in Mr. Seppeld's place I would do precisely as Mr. Seppeld did," said Aunt Prudence.

"Quite the contrary, my dear, quite the contrary. I believe there is a peculiar temptation for each one of us — a temptation to which we would more readily yield than others would. Mr. Seppeld's temptation has, perhaps, come to him, and he has yielded to it. Ours may not yet have come to us. I hope it never may."

"Well," sharply retorted Aunt Prudence, "if it makes me act one-half as mean as Mr. Seppeld has acted — so do I."

"It seems very strange," said Uncle Dan, slowly moving his hands back and forth over his knees, "it seems very strange that both Mr. Brock and Professor Bulbous should be so eager to give their daughters to this young man. Surely the professor cannot have the same reason for desiring Mr. Seppeld as a son-in-law."

"Motive," said Dick, "fear."

"Fear!" exclaimed Uncle Dan.

"What does he fear?" asked Aunt Prudence.

Dick answered with one word, "Exposure!"

"Dick," observed Aunt Prudence, shortly, "no nonsense. Tell us all about it."

Dick inclined his head and complied.

"You remember the serenade?"

"Perfectly, Dick, perfectly," said Uncle Dan. "What execrable music that was, to be sure. But they meant well, and they tried hard."

"Remember, too," asked Dick, "the fire?"

"How can I forget it? What a shabby trick that was! And we never discovered the author of it."

"I did."

"You did! Dear me!"

"Who was it?" asked Aunt Prudence.

"Same party," said Dick; "Seppeld."

Uncle Dan had been softly rubbing his hands. But he now put them back upon his knees and stared at Dick with all his might.

"Of course," said Aunt Prudence, nodding her head as if the news was nothing more than she had expected, "it's in him, and it must come out. But what did he do it for? Go on, Dick."

"Reason," said Dick, "jealousy."

"I declare ——" began Uncle Dan.

"Keep still," Daniel," said Aunt Prudence. "Go on, Dick."

"He was jealous of Bob. Heard there was to be a serenade; thought Bob was the man who intended to bring it; so he bought a lot of gunpowder — put it on the sidewalk — hid behind the fence — intended to touch it off when Bob passed over it. Bob didn't come, and so he touched it off for Cliphart's benefit. I saw him — followed him — cornered him ——"

"Cornered him!" exclaimed Uncle Dan. "Dear me! What does that mean?"

"Why," said Dick, innocently, "I told him I was going to have him arrested."

"Good," was Aunt Prudence's comment. "I hope that brought him to his senses."

"Yes," said Dick, "to his marrowbones. He confessed, told me all about the professor, and the secret of his power over him. I never heard of such a plot. Well, the secret is, Professor Bulbous is an impostor."

"What!" cried both Uncle Dan and Aunt Prudence.

"Fact," continued Dick, with a nod. "He's an impostor; no more Professor Bulbous than you or I. He's a lie, a cheat, a fraud. Seppeld discovered it by accident. That's the secret of his power over the man. Fine business, isn't it?"

For once in his life his favorite expression failed Uncle Dan. He sat dumbfounded, unable to say a word.

"Well," said Aunt Prudence, briskly, "that's news, surely. But how shall he be exposed?"

"He's exposed already," said Dick, producing a letter from his pocket, "this letter from him to Seppeld tells the whole thing. It was found the next day after the serenade by Cliphart, near the fence where Seppeld hid that night. Cliphart couldn't read it — called in Brankey — Brankey read it — spread the news among a few friends — it spread further — all up town knows it, and it will be in the morning papers."

"Well — well — well — well!" slowly exclaimed Uncle Dan, "never in the whole course of my life have I heard of such extraordinary occurrences as have happened right around me in the last few days. To think that I intended to ask that man to do me the favor to allow Bob to visit Bella without interruption, and marry her if she preferred him! Dear me! I have no doubt he would have refused me — no doubt of it whatever."

Dick smiled and Aunt Prudence coughed.

Uncle Dan opened his mouth as if to speak again, when he was interrupted by a violent ringing of the front-door bell.

"Gracious!" exclaimed Aunt Prudence, surprised into an exclamation by this unexpected alarm, "what's that?"

The door was no sooner opened, a service which Dick had quietly performed, than Mr. Harry Cribbler burst into the room in a state of the greatest excitement — his face flushed — his hands waving above his head, while he cried, in a tone of wild entreaty, "Uncle Dan! Uncle Dan! Come — come quick!"

Uncle Dan sprang to his feet.

"Dear me! What is the matter, Harry?"

"Bob!" cried Harry — "he's gone down there — to fight the professor. I mean, the other man, not the professor. Professor Bulbous, you know; the man that was Professor Bulbous, but he's somebody else now, you know. Oh, hurry! If you want to prevent bloodshed, Uncle Dan — come right away — Come quick!"

There was no resisting this appeal. Indeed, at the first intimation of danger to one of his friends, Uncle Dan had run for his hat, and as Harry paused for breath, he was ready to accompany him.

Dear, benevolent man! Who, seeing him hurrying along the street between excited Mr. Cribbler and cool Mr. Doolittle, his arms regularly moving to and fro as he walked, his sturdy limbs now keeping time with Mr. Doolittle's long strides, now with Mr. Cribbler's shorter steps, and anon with neither, while his face, over an expression of fatherly concern and apprehension, bore a look of determination — determination to rescue Bob, even at the peril of life and limb, from any danger into which he might have rashly plunged — who, seeing

Uncle Dan thus hastening towards Professor Bulbous' house would not have earnestly desired such a friend in time of need?

Surely, surely such a man will live in the affections of his friends forever.

CHAPTER XXXIII.

Which relates how Mr. Sturdy set out to punish the false professor; why he did not do it, and ends with his commendable determination to comfort a young lady.

MEANWHILE Mr. Bob Sturdy, valiant little Mr. Sturdy, steadily tramped toward the professor's house, from an opposite direction, filled with high purpose and ennobling thought, and with that air of positiveness and resolve which had ever distinguished that small-statured, but great-spirited artist. And as Mr. Sturdy thus unswervingly pursued his way, now and then striking the air several times in rapid succession with a cowhide, and unconsciously uttering monosyllabic, albeit unintelligible threats, it was a sight which ought to have inspired the respect, as it certainly did attract the attention, of numerous passers-by, who, stopping for a moment upon their journeys to gaze after the stern-featured little gentleman, wondered what in the world he was up to.

"What!" thought Mr. Sturdy, "has such a man had the audacity to deny me the hand of Bella

Bulbous? Has such a man endeavored to force the girl whose heart is mine into an alliance with a fellow almost as bad as himself? Has such a man had the presumption to compel me to see my girl on the steps, and slammed the door in my face? Have I hung around the street corners like a common loafer in order to see Bella, for such a scoundrel?"

And as such thoughts chased each other through the mind of the brave projector of the picture of Napoleon, the five fingers of his left hand were pushed vigorously through his bushy hair, the five fingers of his right hand grasped the whip more firmly, and the resolved look upon his face deepened into a frown of the greatest magnitude.

In this manner was Mr. Sturdy rapidly nearing the end of his journey when his attention was attracted by a loud noise which proceeded from the centre of a crowd, gathered in the centre of the next block before him. Cautiously approaching, and peeping through such spaces as he could find between the bodies of the members of the gradually increasing assemblage, Mr. Sturdy beheld three gentlemen, two of whom were belaboring a third without mercy, who, as might be expected, was crying, "Watch!" and "Murder!" with might and main.

"You ole reskel!" puffed one stout gentleman, whom the surprised Mr. Sturdy instantly recognized as Mr. Cliphart, "You will foolen uns? You will maken uns believen you is en professor? You will doen dis? Tek dat, en dat, en dat!"

Here at last was the false professor come to justice. Here at last was the object of Bob's vindictive search already in the hands of his chastisers. As Mr. Sturdy continued to look upon the scene he saw, with astonishment, that Mr. Cliphart's assistant was none other than the despised Mr. Brankey.

"Watch! Help! Murder!" cried the exposed impostor, vainly endeavoring to defend himself from the hammer-like blows of the powerful Mr. Cliphart. As for Mr. Brankey, his muscular power having long been impaired by the constant use of stimulants, his efforts only drew upon him the sharp derision of the bystanders.

As Mr. Sturdy, gradually edging his way into the inner circle, looked upon this exciting scene, the valiant purpose which had inspired him left him : for, if the truth must be confessed, the longer Mr. Sturdy beheld this brutal exhibition the more thoroughly ashamed of himself he began to feel, and he soon found himself, instead of glorying in Mr. Cliphart's success, really pitying the dark-haired professor, down whose face the blood was streaming from many an ugly wound.

It was therefore with intense relief that Mr. Sturdy saw the circle rudely broken, and beheld the appearance of two policemen, who, with professional and practised skill tore the struggling trio apart, and promptly marched them to the lockup.

To say that Mr. Sturdy thanked his lucky stars as he slowly sauntered from the spot, would be but feebly to express his joy and gratitude.

But what should he do now?

As if in answer to this question a bright thought entered his mind.

And as it did so a pleased and gratified smile suffused Mr. Sturdy's hitherto serious countenance. Joy sparkled in his eyes, his step grew more elastic, his form was more erect, and he mentally exclaimed, "That's it! I'll call on Bella! She needs comfort, I know she does. Poor girl! She hasn't a soul in all the world to care for now but me!"

And as Mr. Sturdy came to this sad reflection he laughed — he actually laughed.

And turning his face once more in the direction of Professor Bulbous' house, Bob hastened upon his charitable mission.

CHAPTER XXXIV.

Uncle Dan to the rescue. — The story of the false friend. — The mob.

WHILE the three friends thus nobly hastened to the assistance of Mr. Sturdy, Dick related how Mr. Seppeld had discovered that the stout, black-haired gentleman who had been known as Professor Bulbous was not Professor Bulbous, but a stranger who had assumed all the relations of the absent professor, and had imposed upon the public for a period of five years. Briefly told, Mr. Seppeld had intercepted a letter addressed to Miss Bulbous, and post-marked Amsterdam.

This foreign letter proved to be a notice of the death of William Bulbous, only living relative — with the exception of Bella Bulbous — of Claudius Bulbous, deceased, and informing Miss Bella Bulbous that she was the sole heir to a large property.

Professor Claudius Bulbous had, fourteen years previous to this time, arrived in the city of St.

Louis with his wife and one child, a little girl five years of age. In one year from his arrival, his wife faded and died, and was laid to rest in the land of strangers. In another year Professor Bulbous had placed his little girl in a boarding-school and had returned to his native country, the Kingdom of the Netherlands. Some said that he had gone back to find another wife; others, that business connected with his property in the old country required his attention; others, that he had returned to visit the famous musicians of the old world.

Be that as it may, Professor Claudius Bulbous was not heard from again until nine years afterward, when a stranger — having gained admittance to the school where Bella Bulbous had spent her orphaned childhood, announced himself as the long lost musician, and claimed his daughter.

No one questioned his title. In form and feature he resembled Claudius Bulbous so closely that those who had seen the professor — very few indeed there were who remembered him — believed that this was the veritable man.

It is necessary here to say that the real Professor Bulbous had, indeed, returned to Europe to complete his musical studies. In Paris he had formed the acquaintance of, and a strong attachment for, a man whose principal business hitherto had been the building of barricades, (when he was not hiding from the police), and showing his love to his country by shooting down as many of its inoffensive citizens as possible.

Professor Bulbous confided in this man. And when he was prostrated by disease and lay dying far away from all his relatives and friends, he charged this man to take his love to his little daughter in far away America, and to bring her home to Holland. He told him furthermore, that he was one of the heirs to a large property in Leyden and in Amsterdam: that a dispute between William Bulbous, his brother, and himself had terminated in a lawsuit; and begged the communist to protect his daughter's interests. The false friend promised to do everything required of him, and soon thereafter Professor Claudius Bulbous died.

No sooner was the professor buried than the deceiver formed a bold plan to enrich himself at the expense of Bella Bulbous and at the cost of his own honor. He determined to personate the professor, and hoped, if the lawsuit should be eventually declared in favor of Claudius Bulbous, to deceive even the sharp eyes of a defeated and angry relative and of the law.

But the relative was not to be so easily deceived.

His spies had informed him of the death of his brother. And while the false Bulbous was still upon his way to the West the proof of the death of the real Bulbous was presented to the court and judgment obtained in favor of the living man.

The false professor had been informed of this decision and had made claim in the name of Bella Bulbous. In the meantime William Bulbous died, and the property so long in dispute was at length declared to belong to Miss Bella Bulbous. The letter apprising Miss Bella Bulbous of this decision coming into Mr. Seppeld's hands, that worthy conceived the notion of marrying Miss Bulbous; and by threats of exposure and promises of a liberal reward secured the co-operation of the false professor in his plans. Although Mr. Seppeld had first contemplated a union with Miss Brock, that union, in view of Miss Bulbous' altered fortunes, seemed to him no more desirable : yet, appreciating the saying "there is many a slip 'twixt the cup and the lip," Mr. Seppeld shrewdly continued his suit for Miss Brock's hand, with sufficient warmth to deter more honest suitors and deceive the squire himself.

His cowardly confession to Dick Doolittle, and the accidental loss of a letter, in which the false professor, alluding to his imposture, begged Mr.

Seppeld not to expose him, overthrew all his plans.

As Uncle Dan, in company with Harry and Dick, drew near the professor's house, they saw before it a noisy and excited crowd of people, and heard many voices shouting and threatening the professor with dire vengeance.

"Drive him out!" cried one.

"Let us in!" shouted another.

"Where's the counterfeit fiddler?" sneered a third.

"Open the door!" "Break it down!" "Tar and feather him!" "Give him the whip!" "Ride him on a rail!" "String him up!" were the vindictive cries which saluted the ears of Uncle Dan and his two friends.

"Dear me!" exclaimed Mr. Poldertot, "this will never do — never! They must be spoken to."

And so saying Mr. Poldertot darted forward and forced his way through the excited crowd; nay, more — he actually mounted the stairs, and turning, stood in full view of every one, with his face to the people and his back to the door.

CHAPTER XXXV.

The heroic action of Uncle Dan and his friends. — The alarming manifestations in a coal-cellar. — A strange mishap to Mr. Sturdy, succeeded by success and joy. — The last of the old tin-sign.

WHEN Uncle Dan turned and faced the crowd which had gathered before the musician's door, he assumed as stern a look as it was possible for his good-humored countenance to bear, and indignantly demanded to know what they wanted.

It is probable that Mr. Poldertot had never faced an audience of this kind before; and had never, until this moment, had the pleasure of attracting the undivided attention of that unorganized, irresponsible mass of individuals called a mob. Wherefore, we may safely infer that Uncle Dan had never before been greeted with such vigorous and choice salutations as now assailed him.

"Who are you?" "Oh, bag your head!" "Halloa, pudding-face!" "Come down out o' that!" and a variety of like expressions saluted gentle Uncle Dan.

But — we make this assertion with pride and gratification — had a thousand mobs uttered their taunts and execrations Uncle Dan would have faced them all undauntedly. And, inasmuch as the mildest-mannered person will, upon extraordinary occasions, become as strong and as brave as a lion, Uncle Dan, conscious of being upon the side of right, became, figuratively speaking, a man of iron.

"I ask you," cried Mr. Poldertot, growing red in the face with the unusual exertion required to make himself heard, "what do you want? And if there is a gentleman among you, I want him to reply."

A storm of derision again greeted the speaker, during which various epithets and nicknames having especial reference to Uncle Dan's fulness of face and form were bestowed upon him with the most refreshing prodigality.

"I know what you've come for," cried Uncle Dan, shaking his clenched hands at the crowd, and speaking with unaccustomed warmth, "you've come to break the law! You've come to enter a private house and let your unbridled passions loose upon the inmates! Shame upon you, gentlemen; shame upon you!"

"Who is he talking to?"

"Hit 'im wid a rock!"

"Knock him off the steps!"

"Go for 'im!"

"Pull 'im away!"

"Pitch into him!" were a few of the angry cries which now arose from the mob, while it began to surge and move more wildly every moment, drawing nearer and nearer to Uncle Dan, with arms raised and clenched hands shaking threateningly.

Not for an instant did Uncle Dan quail. Hastily turning back his sleeves above his wrists and planting himself more firmly upon the steps, Mr. Poldertot rapidly revolved one chubby fist around the other as a token of defiance, and cried, "Come on! Come on! A parcel of cowards! A pack of knaves! I'm ready for you! Come on, and touch me if you dare!"

And as Uncle Dan stood there with his feet wide apart, his stout body braced against the door, his usually good-humored face red with indignation, his fists performing rapid and continuous revolutions one around the other, and his whole attitude expressive of the greatest valor and defiance, it was a sight that would have challenged the respect and admiration of any persons except the members of this angry mob.

"Come on!" cried Uncle Dan once more, "come on!"

The crowd was close around him, and as Uncle Dan uttered this last remark a robust, lusty-voiced individual advanced, crying, "We've had enough o' you, old man — come out o' that!" and put forth his hand to grasp Uncle Dan's arm.

But before the hand touched him and before Uncle Dan could defend himself his assailant was suddenly repulsed by a blow that sent him staggering back into the arms of his friends. Another who had advanced to attack Uncle Dan from the other side, was similarly received, while a third, who rashly advanced in front and had actually mounted two of the steps was so warmly welcomed by a set of hard, unmerciful knuckles that he promptly tumbled from the steps and lay upon the pavement groaning, "Oh, my eye! My head! I'm killed — I'm killed!"

The mob, arrested by this unlooked-for catastrophe, stared in blank amazement at the steps where this incident had occurred; and beheld, standing before Uncle Dan, a strong, broad-shouldered young man, immovable as a statue and silent as the grave. And nothing but his clenched hands, held before him in a position of scientific defence, and his keen, watchful eyes, indicated that this was the gentleman who had so ably defended Uncle Dan.

"Dear me! Dear me!" said the astonished and grateful Mr. Poldertot. "That was nobly done, Dick; nobly done. I declare, I had forgotten all about you."

At that moment a young man wildly brandishing an iron dray-pin, sprang forward and took up a position beside Mr. Doolittle.

"Well—well! And you, too, Harry!" exclaimed Uncle Dan, "Dear me! Who next? who next?"

"Police! Police!" cried Mr. Harry Cribbler, beckoning frantically with the left hand while he brandished his novel weapon with his right, "Come and arrest half a dozen of these fellows for disturbing the peace!"

At this alarming cry those who had been foremost and noisiest crept through the crowd to its outskirts, and vanished in the darkness.

With the disappearance of the ringleaders, the vacilating, cowardly mob lost its power of adhesion; and, separating into its component parts, dribbled away in all directions.

The full beauty of Mr. Cribbler's bright idea will be appreciated when it is known that he could not see a single guardian of the peace within the range of his vision. The police was simply a product of Mr. Cribbler's excellent imagination.

Thus do novelists continually impose upon the world for verities their baseless fictions; and frighten us from day to day with shadows.

"And now," said Uncle Dan, when the rabble had oozed away, and the street was comparatively clear, "where's Bob?"

Ah, true enough! Where was Bob, to be sure? What had become of him? And why had he not shown himself during the progress of the exciting scenes which had just transpired? It was an unanswerable conundrum. And the greatest apprehension and fear began to trouble Uncle Dan regarding the safety of their valorous but diminutive friend.

"Dear me!" exclaimed Uncle Dan, "I hope nothing unpleasant has happened to Bob." Then he descended the stairs, and turning, gazed long and earnestly at the blank walls and closed doors and windows of the row.

"What shall I do?" he said — "what shall I do?"

"Suppose we ask somebody about him. Miss Bulbous, for instance."

And as this sensible suggestion fell from Dick's lips, Uncle Dan nodded his head quickly, and responded, "True, true, Dick; and how dull of me not to have thought of that before."

And then Uncle Dan hurried toward the house, and, mounting the stairs which he had just descended, knocked at the door. The row could not afford the luxury of that modern tinkling innovation, a door-bell.

Upon hearing the knocking Miss Bella Bulbous, who, peering through the shutters, had been a thoroughly frightened but now joyful spectator of all that had occurred, hastened to the door and opened it.

"Oh, Mr. Poldertot," exclaimed Miss Bulbous, "those awful men!"

As Miss Bulbous accompanied this exclamation with a gasp, and began to show symptoms of weakness, Uncle Dan put forth his arms to hold her.

"Dear me!" thought that good man, "she's going to faint!"

Then speaking aloud, he said, "It's all right, my dear — it's all right."

"Oh, my poor papa!"

Now as Uncle Dan did not know whether she referred to the real or the false parent he did not know precisely what to say — and like a wise man, as he was, said nothing, but stared helplessly at the fair charge in his arms.

"To think that he should die so far away from me in that horrid frog country! And I never knew it!"

"It was sad, my dear," replied Uncle Dan, sympathetically, "but don't cry, my dear, don't cry. And so you know the whole story?"

"Yes — and I thought this man was my father, and now I'm all alone in the world, Mr. Poldertot, all alone!"

"Dear me!" thought Uncle Dan, "now she's going to have hysterics."

"Never mind," he said, reassuringly, "I'll be your friend, my dear, and nobody shall harm you. But don't faint, Miss Bulbous, don't faint, I beg of you. Because I want to ask you — are you listening? — whether you have seen Bob — Mr. Sturdy, I mean — and, dear me! what's that?"

Uncle Dan's blood curdled within him, while Miss Bulbous, startled out of all disposition to faint, clung to his arm in terror, as a shriek such as had never before greeted their ears, echoed and re-echoed through the hall, succeeded by a second and a third, equally loud and piercing.

"Oh-h-h!" screamed Miss Bulbous.

"What can that be?" cried Uncle Dan.

"That's a woman," said Dick.

"And she's being killed," added Harry.

"Here, Dick, take care of Miss Bulbous," cried Uncle Dan, releasing himself and running through the hall to the back door.

"Harry, stay here a minute, will you?" said Dick, and followed Uncle Dan.

Harry looked as if he would cheerfully have given Miss Bulbous in charge of another gentleman. But the fair lady held his arm with a determined grasp.

"Oh, Mr. Cribbler, don't leave me."

Mr. Cribbler looked wistfully at the back door, assured her that the idea of leaving her was furthest from his thoughts, and begged her to compose herself, at the same time quietly suggesting that they might as well follow their friends and see what the trouble was. And as Miss Bella Bulbous tremblingly signified her willingness to act upon this suggestion they walked toward the back door.

"Oh, Mr. Cribbler, don't," cried Miss Bulbous, as Harry's hand touched the door-knob, "don't open the door!"

"But we can't see anything if we keep it closed," retorted Mr. Cribbler, and opened it without more ado.

And as they stood in the doorway and looked out into the yard, they beheld Uncle Dan and Dick, listening to a woman whose wild eyes, frowzy hair, and excited manner gave her the appearance of having just been frightened out of her senses, and around whom were gathered a highly interested circle of neighbors.

The woman held a coal-hod in one hand and a lantern in the other, with which she made sudden motions toward a sloping cellar-door near by.

"An' I kem out o' the house wid me coal-bucket in me hand, an' just as I kem near the duur I heard a sound, quare-like, under the duur; but I didn't think nawthin' o' that, zir, naw, zir,—I didn't until I wint for to lift up the duur, when all at wanst I saw a black head—an' a pair o' fiery eyes a comin' up out o' the cellar at me, zir—yis, zir—an' the like o' that same I niver seen before, zir, naw, zir; an' oh! it tuk me breath away that clane that I cud do nawthing but scrame, zir."

"She's seen a ghost," said a fat woman, rolling her eyes.

"It is my opinion," said a lean, extraordinary tall, and serious-looking lady, "that she saw the evil one."

"An' his mouth was open, zir, an' fire was a comin' out of it, zir, an' I thawt I was dead—shoore, so I did, zir."

"But, my dear woman," said Uncle Dan, "what did you do then?"

"Thin I shut the duur, zir — an' locked it — an' I belave I hit him on the head, bekase I heard him a groanin' like he was kilt, an' thin I screamed agin, zir, an' thin you coome, zir."

"I'm not going to live here another day," said the fat lady.

"It is my opinion," said the tall, serious lady, "that the place is infested with spirits."

"I knowed it — I knowed it," exclaimed a short, broad, chubby, German lady, "I always suckspected dat somedings was wrong mit de cellar. All my krout is spoilt. Un' dat is a werry bat sign."

"And when I went for water," chimed in a servant girl, "I heard the dismallest moanings — you wouldn't believe! And then something said, 'Help! Help!' And, oh! I was so scared. I run away as fast as I could."

"And I'd just been in the cellar," added another servant girl, "and got two buckets of coal. And after I'd taken one bucket up-stairs I came down after the other. And when I went to lock the cellar-door something thumped against it from the inside. I thought I should die!"

"And have none of you," inquired Uncle Dan, "had the courage to go into the cellar and see what this means?"

The horrified looks which followed this question were a sufficient reply.

"It is my opinion," said the serious lady, "that the gentleman is beside himself."

"It is my opinion," retorted Uncle Dan, "that you have all been frightened by your own imagination. What do you say, Dick?"

"I say," replied Dick, "rats."

"Or," suggested Harry, from the doorway, "cats."

"Or," said Uncle Dan, "some one is locked in and can't get out. Lend me the key, madam, and we will soon unravel this mystery. Come, Dick."

As Uncle Dan advanced and placed the key, which the frightened woman had given him, in the lock, a sudden thumping took place as of some one striking against the inner surface of the cellar-door with a hard, heavy substance.

The bravest of the women formed a circle around Uncle Dan and Dick, while the feeble-hearted looked on in fearful expectation from a distance.

Turning the key in the lock and suddenly throwing open the doors, Uncle Dan was instantly petrified with astonishment.

Dick took one long look, puckered his mouth as if to whistle, and then suddenly collapsing, burst into such a loud and continuous roar of laughter as no one who knew him would have deemed him capable of; while Harry had no sooner glanced into the open cellar than he sat down upon the doorstep at Miss Bulbous' feet, placed his hands on his sides, beat a complicated tattoo upon the ground with his heels, and laughed until the tears came into his eyes and rolled over his cheeks.

And while they were thus affected, there slowly and painfully clambered out of the cellar, over the coal-heap, with the most woe-begone expression and crestfallen air, and with his face, hands, shirt-front, and collar so blackened with dust and coal-dirt, and decorated with cobwebs as to render him almost unrecognizable, that valiant hero, that great artist, that positive friend — Mr. Robert Sturdy.

And we may truthfully say that never had Mr. Sturdy, through all his unfortunate adventures, appeared to so great a disadvantage as at that moment.

When it was actually proven that Mr. Sturdy was flesh and blood, and not an apparition, the natural result was a suspicion in the minds of the ladies that Bob was a burglar, or thief, or other obnoxious character, which suspicion manifesting itself in dark and threatening looks, and audible expressions in addition to the grave remark of the serious lady, "I am of the opinion that this individual is a purloiner. He ought to be delivered to the police authorities," aroused Uncle Dan to the importance of doing something to protect and exonerate his young friend.

"Bob," said Uncle Dan, "how did you get in there?"

"I fell in there," said Bob, gloomily.

"You fell in?"

"Yes. The cellar-door was open. I didn't notice it. I stumbled over a coal-hod and tumbled in. And when I tried to get out I found the door locked."

"My dear boy," said Uncle Dan, his ready sympathy instantly aroused, "that was too bad. But how in the world did you get into the back-yard? Why did you not go to the front-door?"

"There was a mob in front," said Bob, "and I was afraid they would break into the house and harm Miss Bulbous. I knew I couldn't get in through the front door while that crowd was there, and so I came around the back way. I wanted to help Miss Bulbous to escape."

Miss Bulbous, hearing these words, retreated into the hall, and there addressing the blank wall, exclaimed, "Oh, you dear fellow!"

"You see," said Uncle Dan, turning to the

circle of neighbors, and waving his hand, while his countenance was illuminated with one of its happiest smiles, "you see, my friends, how even the best of intentions may sometimes lead us into misfortune. I can assure you that my young friend here — Mr. Robert Sturdy, at your service — is as honest and as true as the day is long; and if you never have a worse man to deal with you will be — it affords me the greatest pleasure to say it — very fortunate, indeed."

Having uttered this unqualified recommendation, Uncle Dan drew his arm through Bob's and led him into the house. And soon, with the assistance of his friends, and a plentiful application of soap and water and brushes, Bob was in a fairly presentable condition.

And now, while Uncle Dan and his three young friends were gathered together in Miss Bulbous' parlor, that young lady, overflowing with gratitude for the great services rendered, bustled about in the greatest haste to make tea; and in an incredibly short space of time had five cups of that favorite beverage smoking hot upon the table. And while enjoying this fragrant refreshment (which Uncle Dan privately assured Dick, was as excellent as any that Aunt Prudence had ever made), explanations of all that had occurred took place, during which Uncle Dan delivered a perfect avalanche of "Dear me's!" and "Well — well's!" while Harry mentally jotted down a number of items for insertion in that mysterious and never finished "Great American Novel."

"Now," said Uncle Dan, putting down his empty cup for the second time, "if I don't hurry home, Prudence will be after me with a sharp stick. You know, my dear, she naturally feels a little anxious about me. And when I'm out late — oh, well — you will appreciate her feelings some of these days."

And then Uncle Dan bestowed such a significant look upon Miss Bulbous and Mr. Sturdy that the lady blushed, and Bob looked only a trifle less foolish than when he emerged from the cellar.

In her most winning manner Miss Bulbous besought Uncle Dan to stay a little longer, pleading that it was not very late and that he might oblige her, as this was his first visit.

But Uncle Dan, with the fear of Aunt Prudence in his mind, resisted all persuasion.

"No — no," he said, smiling pleasantly, "you have three young gentlemen to entertain and that is enough. Let me go home. You don't want an old man here."

"Mr. Poldertot," exclaimed Miss Bulbous, "you will *never* grow old."

Oddly enough, Uncle Dan no sooner moved toward the door than Dick and Harry both followed. And without giving any clear reason for their sudden departure, hastened away with that estimable gentleman and staunch friend.

"Uncle Dan," said Dick, in gloomy disgust, as they slowly sauntered homeward, "it's all up!"

"It's all up!" echoed Uncle Dan, struck more by Dick's peculiar tone than by the words he had uttered, "What's all up?"

"Why," said Dick, moodily, "freedom, happiness, single-blessedness, everything; all gone to the dogs."

"My dear boy," said mystified Uncle Dan, "you know how hard it is for me to understand anything but the simplest language. Not that I mean to say that you do not express yourself intelligibly, Dick. Nothing of the sort. But if you could say the same thing in some other way — a little more openly — that is, so I can see it — more — ah — more — oh, dear me! You know what I mean."

Dick stopped on a street-corner under a gas-light, which shone upon his face, whereby Uncle Dan saw that he had one eye closed and the other half-open.

"I mean," said Dick, "that Bob's going to throw himself away to-night. And that is the end of us. This is my way, sir, and that's yours. Good night."

And without offering any further explanation of his meaning, Dick suddenly closed the eye that was open and opened the eye that was closed, and sped away.

Harry courteously held out his hand. "Good night, Uncle Dan."

"Ah — oh! yes — yes; you turn down that way. But tell me, Harry, what Dick means."

"Dick means," said Harry, "that Bob will probably propose to Miss Bulbous this evening."

"Why, so he may, so he may. And an excellent girl she seems to be — very like Prudence when I first knew her. Do you think she will take him, Harry?"

"Undoubtedly," said Harry, "she likes him very much, indeed."

Uncle Dan wrung Harry's hand with the greatest vigor, and said, "Good! good! And I wish them all prosperity and joy. And may you, Harry, and Dick, also, soon follow his example. Good night, my lad, good night; and pleasant dreams."

At this moment a slight breeze beginning to stir along the streets, hunts through the silent thoroughfares until it finds the old tin sign, which now hangs like the useless banner of a defeated army, upon its rusty rod, and setting it in motion, produces from that inharmonious instrument a series of harrowing and discordant sounds.

Bob looks at Bella; and Bella looks at Bob. For this familiar sound recalls a host of memories. And in those memories all its discordance is forgotten, and it becomes at once the sweetest music they have ever heard.

"Bella!" says Bob; and he takes her hand; for he has grown suddenly quite bold; while Bella, usually so self-possessed, blushes and looks down. "Bella, may I say now what I have so often tried to say and failed — so often attempted and had no courage to continue — under that old sign — when I dared not enter here? May I tell you, dearest, what has been upon my heart so long?"

Bella only answers with a glance. But what eyes are not more eloquent than tongues? And Bob understands her.

"Bella, dearest, I love you. Will you be my wife?"

"Oh, Robert!"

That is enough. They understand each other — as men and women have understood each other since the days of Eden — and are very happy.

But now a furious gust (for the wind has grown very strong) strikes the old tin sign and sets it twirling on its staff as if it were demented. Oh, such shrieks! Oh, such dismal wailings! Oh, such wonderful, wild, and ear-piercing screeches! What twistings and turnings — as if it is possessed! What swayings to and fro! What sudden wrenches, now to the east and now to the west! What cries — as if of a child in agony! What grindings — as if it has a soul and is rubbing it off against the tyrant rod that holds it! How it dances — sometimes balancing upon its head — as if some crazy athlete were here performing insane antics at this unseasonable hour — then dashing madly down, as if to break itself into a thousand fragments upon the bricks below, only to be brought up with a wild jerk and a nerve-rasping moan upon the other side!

So it keeps on — waving, quivering, shaking hither and thither — producing the strangest sounds — and growing wilder, madder, more unreasonable every moment. Until at last the wind suddenly twisting around the nearest corner, like the lash of a tornado, catches it and beats it most unmercifully. It twirls three times insensibly around its iron rod and chafes against the rust-worn nail that holds it. The nail can no longer do its duty, being feeble, and breaks in two. And then, with one wild, piercing, and triumphant shriek the old sign flutters from its rod, is caught up by the wind, and goes sailing through the air. Over roofs, and chimney-tops and lamp-posts — over telegraph wires and fences — over trains of cars just coming in and trains of cars just going out — over the levee — over stately steamers lying at their moorings like chained leviathans asleep — and so the old sign sweeps in this most furious gale until it hangs trembling over the centre of the river.

It rests a moment, as if exhausted, on an eddy in the air; the eddy breaks, the wind has lost its hold, and the old sign sweeps with inconceivable swiftness toward the river, strikes the water with its edge, and sinks from the sight of man forever.

CHAPTER XXXVI.

Which is the last of all, and contains the natural conclusion of all that has gone before — namely, the end.

THE story has been written; and the tale may be considered told. But as the painter lingers near his completed picture, still — shading a little here, touching a little there — here bringing out a fond suggestion with a brighter coloring, there hiding with a deft hand a defect that none but a most practised eye could notice — so, and for the same reason, that it is a labor of love, the pen that has been so busy for so many hours past, must write a little longer ere it shall trace upon the last page the magic words — the end.

When those two cronies, Mr. Cliphart and Mr. Brankey, were brought to the police station they frankly acknowledged having been the aggressors and even glared with pride upon the professor's bruised and battered face, Mr. Cliphart stoutly maintaining that the impostor richly deserved his punishment, and more, too. The sergeant taking a somewhat different view of the matter, Mr. Cliphart and his friend were placed under lock and key to answer, when the court should please, to a charge of assault and battery. But when the case was called the prosecuting witness failed to appear, and, though diligent search was made for him, could not be found. Nothing was ever heard of him again, and it was accordingly surmised that he had returned once more to his native city, the beautiful Paris, to build barricades and shoot down unoffending citizens.

Mr. Cliphart and Mr. Brankey were accordingly released with a nominal fine and a reprimand for "breach of the peace," and were solemnly warned not to attempt to take the law into their own hands again. And it gives the chronicler great pleasure to state that the warning has been heeded — that Mr. Cliphart and Mr. Brankey have not again engaged in sanguinary onslaughts upon unsuspecting individuals.

By Uncle Dan's efforts Mr. Brankey was induced to become an inmate of an inebriate asylum, and, although not thoroughly reformed, is considerably less of a toper than formerly. Uncle Dan is untiring in his efforts in his behalf, and has talked so much about him that Aunt Prudence has taken hold in the good work. And when Mr. Brankey now gets off upon one of his relapses he is brought to with an energy which almost takes away his breath. He stands in mortal fear of Uncle Dan's sharp-tongued lady, and regards her with the most profound respect. Wherefore there can be no doubt that there is hope for Mr. Brankey still.

Jimmy grew up under Uncle Dan's benevolent care into a smart, bright, active youth, and now occupies Miss Brock's place in the establishment, with a fair prospect of some time becoming the Co. of the firm, thereby changing that innocent delusion into an actual fact.

Mr. Bromley and Mr. Seldon pursued the uneven tenor of their way, until the necessity of earning a living forced them to seek some constant occupation. And in the course of time Mr. Bromley developed into the pompous, deep-voiced freight-agent of a celebrated railroad line. He is generous in his rough, hearty manner, and the "boys" all like him very much, indeed. But there is something of the old Mr. Bromley about him still; and when a slight, spare gentleman, who is the city editor of a daily paper, comes noiselessly into the office and jogs Mr. Bromley's elbow, or pushes his hat over his eyes, or otherwise annoys him, the dignified Mr. Bromley astonishes his visitors by suddenly springing up, vaulting over the office-railing, and dashing after Mr. Ben Seldon with a vigor that looks remarkably like old times ; and if he is so fortunate as to catch that irrepressible individual, pummels him until he cries for quarter. Nevertheless they are the best of friends living, and regularly visit each other twice a week, for they are married — and the population is increasing.

Bob Sturdy and Bella Bulbous were quietly married. Combining business with pleasure, they travelled on their wedding tour toward the city of Amsterdam. Here the necessity of personally attending to the settlement of the Bulbous affairs, including the claims of the courts and the lawyers, detained them in the city for a period of six months, after which they spent three years in travelling through the European states — and now, living in the city where they were married, are as cosy a little couple as one would wish to see.

Failing as an artist — notwithstanding his determination to be a great painter — Mr. Sturdy turned his attention to merchandise, and is one of the most prosperous merchants in the city. In this new relation his positiveness is considered an excellent business trait, and he has become so popular — especially on 'change — that his name is being freely used in connection with the candidacy for the mayor's office — an office in which a little positiveness and independence are sometimes sadly needed. And should he be nominated — as no doubt he will be — he will surely be elected.

When Bob was married the groomsman was Mr. Harry Cribbler, and the bridesmaid was a graceful, dark-eyed lady, a leader of the Band of Hope, a bosom friend of Miss Bulbous, the same who has once before been mentioned in these pages, and whose name was Ella Trigg. The ceremony having taken place in Miss Bulbous' house, which was not far from Miss Trigg's home, and it being withal a very quiet wedding, it was not deemed necessary to have any carriages; and so, late at night, under a sky clear of every cloud, and decorated with its unnumbered stars, Harry Cribbler happily escorted the bridesmaid home. But there was one star brighter than any of the rest. It was the evening star. "Ah," said Mr. Cribbler, his voice growing very tender, "how still, how clear, how beautiful the night is!"

"Very beautiful, indeed," assented Miss Trigg.

"And what thoughts such a sight as this awakens! See the host of stars! And, Ella, there is one more brilliant, more beautiful than all the rest. If the stars were future habitations, and

I could choose my own, I should select that bright, pure evening star."

"No, that is mine," said Miss Trigg, half playfully, half earnestly, "for I have always loved it."

"Ella," said Harry, and his eye was very tender and his voice was very low, "you call it your star and I call it mine. Let us call it ours together."

He took her hand, which rested on his arm, and held it, and it was not withdrawn.

"Yes, dear Ella; and in future let everything — like this bright star — be ours in common."

And underneath that star-besprinkled dome there were that night no happier hearts than these.

Dick, in a spasm of disgust at what he considered the desertion of his two companions, suddenly left the city, without even bidding Uncle Dan "good-bye" (a circumstance which greatly affected that kind-hearted gentleman), and was absent many days.

But one fine, cold winter's morning there came into Uncle Dan's store, a gentleman and a lady. The lady was closely veiled. The gentleman was Dick.

"Dear me! Dear me!" cried Uncle Dan, joy and welcome sparkling in his eyes and shining from his smiling, ruddy face — "how do you do, Dick? Where have you been? I declare, I'm delighted to see you. What in the world have you been doing all this time, my boy; and where have you come from?"

"Uncle Dan," replied Dick, with a curious look f triumph, "I'm revenged!"

"Revenged!" exclaimed Uncle Dan, "Revenged! why, on whom, pray?"

"On Bob," answered Dick.

"On Bob!"

"And on Harry."

"On Harry!"

Uncle Dan evidently gave it up. And leaning on the counter with his elbows as he stood against it with his back, folded his hands before him and regarded Dick with a look which meant as plain as words could have made it, "I can't fathom it, my boy, I can't fathom it. But, no doubt, you'll make it perfectly clear by and by."

"Bob fell in love," said Dick, abruptly.

That being a simple assertion which could be easily comprehended, Uncle Dan nodded his head, and said, "Yes."

"And Harry followed his example."

"Yes," said Uncle Dan, again.

"And then they were married."

Uncle Dan assented once more, mentally wondering what his young friend meant.

"And they didn't ask your advice nor mine about it."

"Well—no," said Uncle Dan, "I can't say that they did. But why should they?"

"Why should they!" exclaimed Dick, with comical indignation, "Haven't you been a father to them? Haven't I helped them out of hundreds of scrapes? And shouldn't they have taken care of themselves and not tumbled head over heels in love, and leave you and me out in the cold? Why did they want to get married? And what's to become of us now?"

"But, my dear boy," replied Uncle Dan, in all earnestness, "they could not help falling in love with such charming young ladies. And their marriage followed as a matter of course."

"Well," said Dick, "I'm revenged."

There was a merry twinkle in Dick's eye; but dear old Uncle Dan looked upon it as a spark of anger. And accordingly felt quite distressed.

"Dear me! Dear me!" said Mr. Poldertot, apprehensively, "what have you done, Dick—what have you done?"

"Why," exclaimed Dick, with a sudden burst of laughter, "*I fell in love!*"

"You fell in love!" slowly echoed Uncle Dan.

"Yes, sir," replied Dick, evidently taking intense delight in the effect produced upon Uncle Dan by this information, "I fell in love."

Uncle Dan's glance involuntarily fell upon the veiled lady. But he said nothing. But Dick, advancing toward the lady took the singular liberty of putting his arm around her.

"And then," said Dick, repeating Uncle Dan's words and smiling very strangely, as if he had another surprise in store for that easily astonished gentleman, "my marriage followed as a matter of course. Uncle Dan let me introduce you to an old friend. Mr. Poldertot — my wife."

And so saying, Dick raised the veil.

And as a happy, rosy, blushing face was disclosed to Uncle Dan's view, the climax of astonishment came upon him, and he sank into a chair, exclaiming, "Miss Wright!—I mean—Miss Brock! Well — well — dear me — dear me! Who would have thought it!"

"I hope you will forgive us, Mr. Poldertot," said Mrs. Doolittle, "for not telling you before. But Dick insisted on surprising you and would not let me write."

"No cards," said Dick, "what's the use? It's

all nonsense, anyhow. But it's all right now, sir. Uncle Dan, salute the bride!"

And as Uncle Dan arose and performed this agreeable ceremony with a grace that would have become an ancient cavalier, and then welcomed and congratulated them and wished them joy and prosperity and long life, the tears of happiness and gratitude came into his eyes, and he concluded, " My boy, my boy — for you and Bob and Harry must never cease to be my boys — I was afraid that I had lost you. But you have come back, and brought me, I trust, a daughter. The circle is not broken, Dick, but is enlarged, as it should be. The chain is rendered stronger, my dears, by the new links that have been added to it. May you be thankful for the new happiness that it has brought you. And as you enter upon a wider and a better sphere of usefulness, may you do so with an earnest desire to live good and noble lives; ever with an humble trust and an earnest faith in Him who is the giver of all good. God bless you all."

Upon the failure of his schemes, Mr. Seppeld left the city; and was last heard from in the far west as a speculator in silver mines; where, having acquired an unenviable reputation on account of certain questionable transactions, he found it quite desirable to depart; which he did so suddenly that in his haste he forgot to leave his future address — a lapse of memory which greatly irritated the sheriff of the county, who to this day is firmly of the opinion that Mr. Seppeld was so very ungentlemanly and discourteous as to purposely depart in order to avoid him.

As for the picture of Napoleon and the Great American Novel, "the least said soonest mended."

Suffice it to say, that neither of these great works were ever completed. Bob does not remember when he last saw the canvass upon which his hopes for fame were fixed. But there is a dim tradition in the Sturdy family that the picture — or rather the faint outline of a picture — lies somewhere in the garret among a mass of rubbish that has not been explored for years.

Thus do our ambitions ofttimes ignominiously fail. Harry still clings to his pet idea; and continually gathers items and studies characters for that great work for which the American nation has been waiting so long and which has not yet appeared. But when it does appear — let all the nations wonder; for it shall be a grand and glorious work, indeed.

Uncle Dan and Aunt Prudence are honored guests in the homes of their young friends; and are really treated more like father and mother than as strangers. They frequently gather together in one of their homes, for each feels a certain proprietary right in all of them. And upon such occasions you will not find — though you travel from the rising to the setting sun — a merrier, jollier, happier company.

"And now," in the words of the ritual of the Band of Hope, "the time has come for us to part." Who fitter than our gentle hero to bid us all farewell?

Uncle Dan appears once more — and for the last time. One hand is in his bosom, the other is extended as if in friendly greeting. His head is bare and his spectacles pushed above his forehead lie blinking at the ceiling. Upon his ruddy, round, good-humored face there rests a beaming smile, such as only he can show. Glad tears are in his eyes, but they do not hide his kind, benevolent glance ; and his mellow voice, full of charity to all the world, repeats the words which he has spoken to Dick and his young wife, and which the writer echoes with the heartiest good-will to every one who looks upon this page: —

"God bless you all."

By Rev. A. B. EARLE, D. D.

The Morning Hour. For Family Devotions and Private Meditation. Contains a portion of Scripture, with suggestive spiritual Exposition, and a brief Hymn for every Day of the Year. Elegant octavo. Cloth, $2.00; half leather, $2.50; full Turkey, $4.00.

"Its comments are everywhere full of the marrow of the gospel." — *Congregationalist, (Boston.)*

Bringing in Sheaves. The outgrowth of the author's long experience in gospel work. 12mo. Cloth. With steel portrait. $1.25.

"One of the most remarkable books ever given to the public." — *Western Recorder, (Louisville.)*

The Rest of Faith. Shows how the soul may abide in sweet and constant rest in all the care of the daily life. Cloth, 40 cts.; gilt edges, 60 cts.; full Russia, 90 cts.

"Meets the deep longings of the hungry soul." — *Watchman and Reflector, (Boston.)*

Abiding Peace. Has been written to meet the latest difficulties and objections in respect to the doctrine of perfect deliverance from unrest and condemnation, and to enable the Christian to enjoy abiding peace in the daily life. 18mo. Cloth, 50 cts.

Work of an Evangelist. A Review of Fifty Years in the Ministry. Together with The Fiftieth Anniversary Sermon, delivered in Tremont Temple, Boston. Cloth, 25 cts.; paper, 10 cts.

The Title Examined; or, How may I Know I am a Christian? A book for inquirers, and for every Christian who would be sure of his title to heaven. 18mo. Cloth, 25 cts.; paper, 10 cts.

Revival Hymns. Contains those Hymns, with the addition of a few tunes, suited to seasons of special religious effort. Large type and convenient size. Cloth, 25 cts.; paper, 10 cts.; 8vo, leather, 90 cts.

Why Not Now? A searching Tract for the Carelesss and the Anxious. 25 cents per dozen.

Growing, because Abiding. Answers important Questions in regard to the rest of faith. 25 cents per dozen.

Ten Evidences of Conversion; with Ten Questions for Self-Examination. 10 cents per dozen.

*** *Any of the above works mailed, postpaid, on receipt of price. Descriptive Catalogue of our Publications free.*

JAMES H. EARLE, Publisher,
178 Washington Street, Boston, Mass

BOOKS OF TRAVEL, HEALTH, &c.

The Pictorial Cabinet of Marvels. Comprising History, Science, Discovery, Invention, Natural History, Travel, Art, and Adventure. Illustrated with full-page engravings and plates in colors. Large royal octavo. Elegantly bound in magnificent gilt and black sides. Gilt edges. A superb illustrated Gift Book. $2.50.

Grandmamma's Letters from Japan. By Mrs. Mary Pruyn. Illustrated. 16mo. Cloth, $1.00.

Mrs. Pruyn, one of the leading ladies of Albany in social position and benevolent enterprise, is widely known for her work in Japan. These letters should be in every home and Sunday-school library.

"Mrs. Pruyn is a close and intelligent observer." — *Evening Journal, Albany.*

Sketches of Palestine. A Description of Scenes in the Holy Land and the East, all in verse. By Rev. E. P. Hammond. With steel Portraits of Mr. and Mrs. Hammond, the tour having been their wedding trip. 16mo. Cloth, 75c.

"The main features of the long journey are seen as in panoramic views. The book is full of Jesus and the Gospel. Hundreds who would not read a sermon will gladly read this, though it is full of sermons." — *Christian News.*

Travels in Bible Lands. By Rev. Emerson Andrews. 6mo. 17 illustrations. Cloth, 8?c.

Contains letters written by Mr. Andrews during one of his visits to the Lands of the Bible. Talks on religious subjects are interspersed. The work is suited specially to youthful readers.

Tact, Push and Principle. By William M. Thayer. 12mo. 370 pages. Cloth, $1.50.

A book for every young man. Gives the elements, principles, and methods of success. Shows that character and success are not in opposition, and illustrates its points and suggestions from the lives of successful men, showing how they succeeded, and inspiring every young man to make the very most of himself.

The Human Body and Health. By E. Small, M.D. 12mo. 432 pages. Illustrated. $1.50.

A book that should be in every household, and with which old and young should become familiar. It treats of the body and the functions and use of its many parts, the laws of health, &c., and all from the standpoint of a Christian physician.

⁎* *Any book mailed, postpaid, on receipt of price. Catalogue of our publications free.*

JAMES H. EARLE, Publisher,

178 Washington Street, Boston, Mass.

MISCELLANEOUS.

* **Complete Poetical Works of James A. Martling.** Illustrated. 12mo. 625 pages. Full Turkey, gilt edges, $5; silk cloth, $2.50.

Prof. Martling writes with exquisite grace and beauty, touching the very finest chords.

"I think the Professor's verses very beautiful, and the lines exquisitely finished." — WENDELL PHILLIPS.

Hon. WM. E. GLADSTONE, England's Prime Minister, said of his translation of Homer's Iliad, "It seems to me to do him great credit."

Pictorial Museum of National History. Including Descriptions of Countries, Peoples, Sports, Adventures, &c., as well as National History. Illustrated with nearly 150 Engravings and Colored Plates. Magnificently bound in silk cloth, covered with designs in gold and black. Large octavo, 508 pp. $2.50. A companion to "Pictorial Cabinet of Marvels."

Between Times. Sketches, Tales, Poems. By I. E. Diekenga, author of "Jasper Groales," etc. 16mo. Elegant cover. 75c.

Mr. Diekenga may be called the Dickens of America, so many of the characteristics of the great English novelist are to be found in his pages

* **History of the Temperance Crusade.** By Mrs. Annie Wittenmyer. Octavo. Over 800 pages. Illustrated. Cloth, $2.50; full gilt, $3; library edition, half morocco, $3.50.

This is one of the most thrilling volumes of the century, and one of the grandest records of honor to woman's consecration, self-sacrifice, and courage. Mrs. Wittenmyer, as a leader of the temperance hosts, has given the public such a book as can hardly be surpassed.

What to Get for Breakfast. By Mrs. M. Tarbox Colbrath. 16mo. $1.

The most unique, helpful, systematic, practical book ever given to the public for making breakfast all it ought to be. In addition to its other matter, more than one hundred bills of fare, with full directions, are given for *home* breakfasts.

The Comparative New Testament. With the OLD and NEW VERSIONS side by side on OPPOSITE pages. Large 12mo. 1000 pages. Extra cloth, red edges, $1.50.

This is decidedly the most satisfactory comparative Testament. In addition to having the versions on opposite pages there is much additional matter, preferred readings, &c.

*** *Any of the above works, except those marked with a star (*), mailed, postpaid, on receipt of price. Books marked *, are sold by subscription. Descriptive Catalogue of our publications mailed free.*

JAMES H. EARLE, Publisher,
178 Washington St., Boston, Mass.

MISCELLANEOUS.

Memorial of Prof. Elihu Root. By Prof. H. H. Neil. Octavo. Paper, 25c.

Prof. Root was one of the purest characters and most promising teachers in science. His life, full of lessons, has been admirably sketched by his friend, Prof. Neil.

London Bridge. A Poem for the Times. By Prof. James A. Martling. 16mo. Illustrated. 40c.

This charming story, in verse, touches upon the relations of labor and capital, as it sketches the lives of its actors.

The Human Will. By Rev. A. B. Earle, D. D. 18mo. Cloth. 25c.

This little work has already been received with most remarkable interest, alike by clergy and laity, and should be everywhere read.

The Old and New Version. By Rev. Philip Schaff, D. D., Chairman of the American Revision Comittee. 12mo. Paper, 10c.

Indian Wars of New England. Including the Life of Eliot, the Indian Apostle. By Colonel R. B. Caverly. 12mo. 476 pages. 16 Illustrations. $2.00.

The heroism and self-denial of the early Pilgrim settlers of New England, in their conflicts with the Indians, furnish lessons that cannot be too often or too strongly enforced. The book is one for the home and the public library.

Pearls of Worlds. By Rev. Emerson Andrews. With Portrait. 12mo. 384 pages. $1.50.

Mr. Andrews adds to his list of works this new volume. It may be styled an ENCYCLOPÆDIA of helps, suggestions, illustrations for preachers, teachers, students, and people generally who wish to get wit and wisdom, personal experience, religious truth, and the like, in compact and ready shape.

"A book of inestimable value."—REV. S. B. WILLIS.

All Things. By Frances Ridley Havergal. Cloth, 25c.; Paper, 10c.

This we regard as one of the most suggestive and helpful of the many works of this very popular author.

⁎ *Any of the above works mailed postpaid on receipt of price. Descriptive Catalogue of our publications mailed free.*

JAMES H. EARLE, Publisher,

178 Washington St., Boston, Mass.

www.ingramcontent.com/pod-product-compliance
Lightning Source LLC
Chambersburg PA
CBHW020231240426
43672CB00006B/487